CLASS AND LIBRARIANSHIP

CLASS AND LIBRARIANSHIP

ESSAYS AT THE INTERSECTION OF INFORMATION, LABOR AND CAPITAL

Edited by

Erik Estep
Nathaniel F. Enright

Library Juice Press
Sacramento, CA

Published in 2016 by Library Juice Press

Library Juice Press
PO Box 188784
Sacramento, CA 95818

http://libraryjuicepress.com

This book is printed on acid-free, sustainably-sourced paper.

Library of Congress Cataloging-in-Publication Data

Names: Estep, Erik Sean, editor. | Enright, Nathaniel F., editor.
Title: Class and librarianship : essays at the intersection of information,
    labor and capital / edited by Erik Estep and Nathaniel F. Enright.
Description: Sacramento, CA : Library Juice Press, 2016. | Includes
    bibliographical references and index.
Identifiers: LCCN 2016018640 | ISBN 9781936117741 (acid-free paper)
Subjects: LCSH: Libraries and society. | Libraries and labor. | Social
    classes.
Classification: LCC Z716.4 .C54 2016 | DDC 021.2--dc23
LC record available at https://lccn.loc.gov/2016018640

Contents

Introduction

Books on class and librarianship have been far and few in between. This is surprising because imprints have been printing volumes on other progressive topics like gender in librarianship, race in librarianship, and intellectual freedom, among others. This volume, *Class and Librarianship: Essays at the Intersection of Information, Labor and Capital,* will hopefully help fill the gap in the literature. Obviously, this is a collection of essays and not an attempt to exhaustively cover the subject. However, there are a wide array of topics, ranging from an essay on the early days of American libraries to some musings on information workers and their possible futures. Appropriately for a book on class, most of the authors rely explicitly or implicitly on Marx. Library and information science faculty and students and working librarians should find something of interest in this volume since the essays include both theoretical and concrete, day to day work.

The first chapter in this volume is Steven Bales clever "The Academic Library as Crypto-Temple: A Marxian Analysis." Borrowing from French Marxist philosopher Louis Althusser, Bales believes that the modern academic library is a religious, communications, cultural, and educational Ideological State Apparatus (ISA), which are designed to uphold and defend the ideological status quo. He thinks that the modern academic library still contains residual religious ideologies and they serve to maintain the hierarchical, capitalist order. This ideology is even inherent in the architecture of modern, academic libraries, which are designed to produce religious awe in their users. This is an original application of Marxist theory to libraries as spaces and deserves further study.

Alexandra Carruthers's "Social Reproduction in the Early American Public Library: Exploring the Connections Between Capital and Gender" looks at the ideology of the public library and finds both supporters of the ruling class and reformers. Carruthers outlines the optimistic ideology of the early women reformers and the ideas of the powerful labor movement and contrasts them with Andrew Carnegie's strong belief in individualism. She also links Melvil Dewey to Carnegie; they both shared a belief in education as a way to solve society's problems. Dewey and other ALA leaders are quoted suggesting that librarianship is uniquely women's work and should be confined to that sphere. Throughout this chapter, Carruthers is sensitive to the challenges reforming women faced against the dominant capitalist ideology. Readers interested in the ideology of the early Public Library Movement should find this chapter illuminating.

Class figures prominently in Amanda Bird and Braden Cannon's "From Steam Engines to Search Engines: Class Struggle in the Information Economy." The authors argue that modern information workers do not have the same strength as resource and transportation workers in the late 19th century, which was an era of great labor power. They make the case that information workers do not actually create information, rather they act as interlocutors that connect users to information. Thus, they don't have the same strength as resource and transportation laborers. The divisiveness of library organizational culture and deprofessionalization also contribute to this weakness. As a way to increase class consciousness, the authors call upon information workers to join with class allies outside of the profession and to organize more within the profession.

In "Working with Information: Some Initial Enquiries," Steve Wright places information at the center of the global, capitalist economy and shows how this affects workers. He analyzes management literature to see how the Information and communications technology (ICT) revolution has impacted the workplace. He also takes a look at scholarship from the workers point of view. Wright finds the increasing automation of ICT as demoralizing workers, with the work becoming banal and routine. He also describes the fragmentation and the division of the workplace. Wright's chapter is more of a literature review and should be useful to information science scholars who are studying information workers.

Toni Samek's contribution, "Crisis Talk," is built upon the key talking points from her closing keynote speech at the Canadian Association of University Teacher's (CAUT) Librarians Conference held in Ottawa, Canada, October 26-27, 2012. The conference theme was "Contested Terrain: Shaping the Future of Academic Librarianship" and operationalized with the question, "Academic librarianship is threatened by Wal-Mart style corporate management that cuts costs by deskilling work, outsourcing professional responsibilities, misusing technology and reducing necessary services and positions. How can our community push back against this destructive agenda?" To put her talk in context, Samek also summarizes the broader conference activity. Although she spoke specifically about Canadian librarianship, her talk can be expanded to universal concerns like class differences in the workplace, faculty and staff relations at libraries, and the class politics of digital labor. She takes some recent Canadian librarian job ads and critiques them for weakening the nature of librarian work and criticizes current LIS education as being potentially harmful to the digital labor movement.

Low-income library users are the focus of Peggy McEachron and Sarah Barriage's "Poverty and the Public Library: How Canadian Public Libraries are Serving the Economically Challenged." The authors highlight the challenges low-income users face in using public libraries such as restrictive fine policies, "library anxiety," and gadget-driven programs aimed at middle class of affluent users. They also review the literature on library services to the poor in the United States and Canada (They include the United States because of the relative paucity of work on Canadian libraries). Outreach efforts like job fairs for the poor and read-a-loud storytimes held in homeless shelters are mentioned. Most interestingly, the authors created a questionnaire designed to get information about programs for the poor in Canadian libraries. They sent it to libraries in the five most populous cities in each of Canada's ten provinces and got twelve responses back. Respondents mentioned services such as free faxes to potential employers, partnerships with homeless shelters, employment support, and adult literacy programs. The authors conclude by urging librarians to make working with the poor their number one priority.

Finally, Carey Sias writes about an often forgotten class of patrons in "Lost in the Gaps: The Plight of the *Pro Se* Patron." Self represented litigants (SRLs) are mostly low income people who can't afford an attorney and decide to represent themselves *pro se*. Sias describes the difficulties they face navigating the often complicated U.S. legal system, the ways in which federal aid initiatives fall short, and where law libraries can fill in the gap. The Legal Services Corporation

(LSC) is the largest funder of civil legal aid programs but affiliates have to turn down half of those seeking help due to lack of resources. Although librarians can't provide direct representation or legal advice they can still help SRLs in many ways. Librarians can provide up to date print and online legal resources, offer guides to legal information, sponsor legal education programming, and even host self-help centers staffed by local law firms. Silas believes libraries should go further and agree to a set of standards to evaluate the services offered and the self-help centers.

Erik Estep

The Academic Library as Crypto-Temple: A Marxian Analysis

Stephen E. Bales

Introduction

Organized religion has been under attack since the Enlightenment period and the development of modern science and secular politics. Dogmatic, objectivist religious beliefs are being challenged by modern knowledge (Cupitt 1984, 8), but religion's mythological legacy lurks in today's secular institutions. The modern academic library is a rather obvious crypto-temple, barely concealing its religious symbolism. This essay is an exploratory venture meant to identify concepts central to the research question: How does the "sacred library" act as ideological scaffolding for capitalism?

I use a Marxian critique to examine the academic library's incorporation of religious elements into its structure, that is, into its matrix of material relations. By applying French Marxist Louis Althusser's concept of the "Ideological State Apparatus" (hereafter referred to as "ISA"), I consider the Western academic library's religious cues.[1] I contend that the modern academic library works as both an educational and a religious ISA. In these capacities, the

---

1   This essay deals with academic libraries in the Western world. While the examination of non-Western information institutions is also important to gaining an understanding of the library as crypto-temple, it falls outside of the scope of this research due to practical constraints. The examination of non-Western academic libraries remains a fruitful area for future research and comparison.

library aids in the reproduction of the social conditions of capitalist production. This chapter concludes with a call for academic librarians to confront the academic library as crypto-temple, to further develop theory concerning the impact of dominant and residual ideologies in academic libraries, and to actively challenge these ideologies.

The Marxian Critique of Religion

Religion remains a contested area in Marxian thought, but an area in need of continual critique. Marx's famous lines from his "Introduction to a Contribution to the Critique of Hegel's Philosophy of the Right" illustrate the differing interpretations that may be applied to Marx's own writings on religion (Newell 1986, 32-3; Raines 2002, 5-6):

> *Religious* suffering is at one and the same time the *expression* of real suffering and a protest against real suffering. Religion is the sigh of the oppressed creature, the heart of the heartless world and the soul of soulless conditions. It is the *opium* of the people.
>
> The abolition of religion as the *illusory* happiness is the demand for their *real* happiness. To call on them to give up their illusions about their condition is to *call on them to give up a condition that requires illusions*. The criticism of religion is therefore in *embryo* the *criticism of that vale of tears* of which religion is the halo. (Marx 1992, 244)

From one perspective, the above view suggests that religion is a potential means of protest (Newell 1986, 33; Sung 2011). But, considering that Marx holds religion as ultimately illusory, and that such illusions, in the end, *do not* support the freedom of humans because they obscure the material relations found in capitalism, Marx's comments concerning religion never amount to more than "faint praise" (Newell 1986, 33). The second part of the above quotation calls for the sober analysis of religion as a means of righting inequitable social relations by unmasking how religion acts as a coping mechanism for enduring exploitation, or, as I conclude in the case of the academic library, an ideological tool for maintaining an exploitative mode of production: an obfuscation maintained by a nominally secular institution.

Nonetheless, one should not read this essay as an indictment of all religion or as a statement concerning the existence of metaphysical reality, but as a critique of a particular implementation of symbols with ideological implications. When critiquing religion as ideology, metaphysical considerations often become irrelevant beyond being used to understand how such metaphysical "realities" influence the historical moment through the maintenance and reproduction of the societal superstructure. Marx said that "the criticism of heaven turns into the criticism of earth, the *criticism of religion* into the *Criticism of law* and the *criticism of theology* into the *criticism of politics*" (1992, 244). The library as crypto-temple, therefore, is not considered here in order to determine its ontological implications, but in terms of its material impact on people that come in contact with it. That is, in how the library patron makes sense of the academic library as crypto-temple, and, in turn, how the library as crypto-temple "makes" the library patron.

THE HISTORICAL ROLE OF THE ACADEMIC LIBRARY AS TEMPLE

For most of recorded history, it was commonplace for Near Eastern and Western academic libraries to be explicitly politico-religious entities. The earliest Egyptian libraries and archives were either attached to temples or were themselves temples, were under the guardianship of scribe-priests, and often served as schools for the reproduction of the scribal class (Wente 1995, 2215-16). For example, the Egyptian library, the "House of Life," was surrounded by statuary of the gods, with the library related deities Thoth and Seshat being especially revered within its walls (Thompson 1962, 3). The libraries of the Mesopotamia and the Fertile Crescent, besides being business archives, were reference libraries for augurs (Arksey 1977, 837). Likewise, early Hellenic archives were typically housed in the Greeks' larger temples (Buchanan 1986, 40).

The Great Library of Alexandria, founded ca. 300 BCE, was arguably the first true university library. It was also the "handmaiden" to the Temple of the Muses (the Museion) to which it was attached, and "indeed its natural complement" (Parsons 1952, 136). The Great Library's "daughter" library, the Serapeum, was itself a temple to the Greco-Egyptian god Serapis (Thompson 1962, 22). In late antiquity, Christian churches housed libraries, and two of the most famous study libraries belonged to Saints Augustine and Jerome (de Vleeschauwer 1963, 148-9). And, despite their greatly diminished stature following the collapse of the Western Roman Empire, European libraries were kept in monasteries or cathedrals, operated by clerics, and collected primarily religious materials (Hessel 1950, 10; Harris 1986, 89-105).

These early library temples helped to maintain the political/economic *status quo*, illustrating the seemingly perpetual connection between religion, politics, and money. Assyriologist A. Leo Oppenheim wrote that a primary function of the Mesopotamian proto-libraries was to maintain the "stream of tradition" to efficiently reproduce the elite scribe-priest class (1960, 411). Mesopotamian library documents served the clients of the institutions in which they were housed, usually a temple or a palace. Therefore, these documents were used to some degree to maintain the administrative structures of the institutions and to preserve the welfare of civilization (Oppenheim 1964, 25-35). Similarly, historians of library and information science have held that the Great Library of Alexandria was created as a tool for supporting the hegemony of the Ptolemaic pharaohs (de Vleeschauwer 1977, 178-81; Erskine 1995, 45).

Only since the Renaissance have Western academic libraries fully embraced concepts of secularity (Jackson 1974, 111-12). This new humanism, in dialogue with developments in economics and the predominant modes of production (i.e., capitalism), politics (e.g., modern social democracy), science (i.e., positivism and post-positivism), and education (i.e., public education), has led to the general disassociation between the concepts temple and library, even for those libraries that collect exclusively religious materials. The modern academic library is portrayed as a workshop for engaging in educational and scholarly research (Cole 1979, 364-385), an organ of modern democracy (Gorman 2000, 161-2), or as a business enterprise (Benton Foundation 1997, 190).

Nonetheless, the sacred characteristics of the modern academic library peek through its secular façade. These religious tells are not "archaic" in the sense defined by Raymond Williams, meaning that they are not always "wholly recognized as an element of the past, to be observed, to be examined, or even on occasion to be consciously 'revived,' in a deliberately specializing way" (2009, 122). Instead, the secular library hides much of its sacredness behind scientific objectivity, covertly combining the currently reigning ideologies—post-positivism and capitalism—with what Williams called the "residual" ideological legacy of past dominant ideologies (122). Although such residual elements may clash with current dominant ideological structures, Williams noted that major residual ideologies are "still active in the cultural process" and are sometimes required for current dominant ideologies to "make sense" of their institutions (122-3). With the academic library, one residual ideology is *the religious*, and an intellectually honest critique of this ideological holdout requires that we put aside romantic notions of the library and consider the effects of this legacy.

The Sacred Aspects of the Secular Library

Nancy Kalikow Maxwell's *Sacred Stacks: The Higher Purpose of Libraries and Librarianship* is one of the first works to make clear the library's contradictory nature as being, at the same time, secular and sacred (2006, 77-93). Maxwell outlined the role of the library as an expression of religion, that is, as a nexus of place and persons serving a "greater purpose" (viii). The thesis of *Sacred Stacks* is that "libraries have survived, and will continue to thrive in the future, because they fulfill eternal needs for people" (viii). In her book, Maxwell advocated that we should keep the library sacred to enhance both individuals and democracy (135). However, as a Marxian analyst, I hold that "eternals" like sacredness and bourgeois democracy reinforce notions of capitalism as natural and inviolable (Marx and Engels 1998, 67-68); bolstering the coercive relationship between dominant and oppressed classes (Marx 1990, 424-25).

Modern libraries, despite claims of secularity, possess symbols that, as will be explained in detail later in this essay, position its patrons ideologically in relationship to the institution. Let us walk through the library in which the present author currently works, Sterling C. Evans Library at Texas A&M University, and identify some of its religious markers. Evans is the main library on Texas A&M's College Station campus, contains its general collection, and serves more than fifty thousand students, faculty, staff, and community users. To get to the library we go to the center of campus, or at least to where the center of campus was when the library was built in 1968. The center is a natural place to find an academic library, as the library is in the middle of most campus's academic lives. The center of things, however, also has

9

religious significance. Anthropologist of religion Mircea Eliade wrote that the temple is a replica of the "cosmic mountain" that resides as a fixed point at the center of the cosmos, ordering the chaos around it (1987, 38), and doing so in the image of "real" or "ultimate" reality. As the seat of knowledge that ultimately orders the life of the University, Evans acts as a hub around which this particular academic cosmos revolves. Go to any college or university campus and you are likely to find the same basic geography: a crypto-temple orbited by enclaves of faculty, students, staff, and the local community.

Approaching Evans, we are impressed by its colossal structure. The library is one of the largest buildings on campus, its massive roof opening up to the sky. Transitions to the sacred are often represented in architecture "by an opening by which passage from one cosmic region to another is made possible" (Eliade 1987, 37). Evans top, therefore, may be read as symbolizing the library's embrace with the ineffable, and in the West, the ineffable is most often associated with a patriarchal god ruling over a hierarchically ordered universe. Similar "interfaces" with the sacred are sometimes represented in architecture by peaks or summits to be ascended, again symbolizing where the mundane meets the eternal (39-41). For an exemplary instance of this latter style of architecture, see the University of Tennessee, Knoxville's John C. Hodges Library, modeled after Mesopotamian ziggurats.

Crossing the threshold of the library, we feel an immediate change in atmosphere. We are now in a crypto-religious space. Despite the community nature of the library's ground floor, a function also shared with religious institutions (Maxwell 2006, 99-101), and despite the fact that Evans library is not hushed in the way stereotypical libraries are portrayed, a noticeable reservation in expression marks the library as different from the street, possibly denoting what David M. Knipe referred to as a "sacred precinct," an "inviolable territory" of the temple (1988, 111). This quiet is a consensual, if primarily tacit agreement to observe a respect for the body of patrons' shared purpose, what Maxwell would recognize as the higher purpose of the library, and what I will summarize as "preserving and creating knowledge for the benefit of humanity." To be silent in the library seems "natural."

Faculty members and students navigate the area, often with an express goal, to encounter and interact with the Holy of Holies, the knowledge contained in the six floors of library shelving. Books, in fact, have a history of designating sacred space and symbolizing a locus of power and authority (Brown 2007, 57; Maxwell 2006, 122). The bibliographic classification systems used by academic libraries to organize these resources, furthermore, harken back to the divinely inspired hierarchies found in Saint Thomas Aquinas's Great Chain of Being.

Meanwhile, Evans's librarians do the same thing that scribe-priests have done for millennia, serving as gatekeepers to the knowledge within the library as well as acting as what Maxwell described as ministers, ascetics, religious scoundrels or respected priests, receivers of confessions, prophets, seers, magicians, and teachers (Maxwell 2006, 21-31). At Texas A&M, the librarians have faculty status and many are tenure track; they work in an organizational structure that culminates in the office of the Dean of Libraries, a patriarchal schema reminiscent of ecclesiastical hierarchies. To access information, patrons often must use the librarians as intermediaries, as cyphers or oracles. Indeed, Evans's librarians act as pseudo-religious specialists that intercede on the patrons' behalf to fully actualize the possibilities of the library *cum* crypto-temple.

Going to Evans, we position ourselves in relation to a hierarchal, crypto-religious ideological institution that is (1) separated from the more manifest examples of library as sacred by a mere few hundred years, and (2) appears to have substituted an eschatological humanism for a service to a god or a monarch (as the representative of a god). We implicitly assume the role of supplicant in relationship to the institution and this goal. How does this happen?

THE ACADEMIC LIBRARY AS IDEOLOGICAL STATE APPARATUS

Althusser's work on ideology remains compelling, particularly his nuanced explanation of the social superstructure's part in replicating capitalism. He provided a means for understanding sociocultural reproduction as a material practice: as a lived integration of the human subject with her ideological landscape and the actualization of her ideologically prescribed part in the prevailing structure of society. When seen through this lens, the academic library becomes ideology *concrète*; its materiality allows the analyst to define the library as an ideological entity and to consider this entity's interior relations, connections with the wider whole of society, and active role in replicating this whole. Furthermore, the academic library as ideology is particularly fascinating in that it possesses facets beyond the educational, including, as argued in the previous section, the religious. Althusser's theories allow the analyst to take this observation, that the library is a crypto-temple, and confront and critique its material effects as a crypto-temple.

According to Althusser, Marxism's base/superstructure model is a useful metaphor in need of elaboration, particularly in terms of the superstructure's role in societal reproduction (2001, 90-1). This idea, that economics is not the sole determinant of social phenomena, requires that the analyst move beyond vulgar Marxian views about the base/superstructure divide. In *For Marx*, Althusser borrowed the concept of overdetermination from psychoanalysis and applied it to sociology (2005, 89-127). In doing so, he recognized the "constitutive complexity" of the superstructure as well as the superstructure's relative autonomy from the base (Elliott 1993, 236). In effect, Althusser merged base and superstructure into a system of relations that acknowledges the complexity of factors that result in the structure of existing "reality," and invites the analyst to identify and understand material instances that contribute to this structure.

This model of reality, what Alex Callinicos described as a unified whole comprised of "related but relatively autonomous instances [e.g., the political system, the educational system]" (1976, 43), rendered obsolete the economic reductionism of Stalinism (Elliott 1993, 236). Althusser's theory, furthermore, provided a basis for the persistence of capitalism and a framework for understanding its reproduction.

In his later work, *Lenin and Philosophy and Other Essays*, Althusser expanded upon Antonio Gramsci's concept of hegemony, that human beings tacitly accept the ideology of the dominant class as a set of rules and limits that structure their range of actions. He did this by explaining how organs of the superstructure act as engines for reproducing capitalism. For Althusser, ideology was the means by which "men represent their real conditions of existence to themselves in imaginary forms" (2001, 110). Ideology exists materially, being embodied in existing institutions and being acted out in material practices. The *raison d'être* of these material practices is to keep the *status quo*, and ideology does this by creating the individual "subject" (explained in more detail in the following section) and incorporating her into its network of social relations. This happens through the encounter between the subject and social institutions, the ISAs.

12

Althusser named several ISAs: the religious, the educational, the family, the legal, the political, the trade union, the communications, and the cultural (2001, 96). These structures work primarily not by coercion, which is the domain of the "Repressive State Apparatuses" (RSAs), e.g., the army, the police, and the judicial system (96), but primarily "*by ideology*" (97). So, although one may be forced by the RSAs to conform—legally or by gunpoint—to the expectations of a society, the ISAs achieve similar results through non-violently conditioning the subject. This indoctrination happens, again, through the ISA as ideology presenting people with the real conditions of their existence "in an imaginary form," i.e., in a form shaped by the society's conventions and put forth as authentic and unalienable. As a result, the real underlying relations between people remain mystified in capitalist phenomena such as the commodity fetish (Marx 1990, 163-177).

In his analysis of Michael Harris's classic "State, Class, and Cultural Reproduction: Toward a Theory of Library Service in the United States," Douglas Raber argued that the public library is an ISA, a "state-maintained, superstructural institution designed not to coerce but to persuade the public of the historical bloc's legitimacy by reinforcing the dominant culture" (2003, 49). The modern academic library is also an ISA, and one that inhabits interesting ideological terrain. It is first and foremost an educational ISA, and, as an educational ISA, it occupies a privileged position (Althusser 2001, 103). In its educational capacity, the academic library reproduces capitalism through supplementing "apprenticeships" to capitalism by which "the relations of exploited to exploiters and exploiters to exploited are largely reproduced" through "the massive inculcation of the ideology of the ruling class" (105-6). This inculcation, through both calculated instruction and immersion in the traditional culture of bourgeois schools, exposes students to the concepts—as well as the appropriate interpretations of these concepts—deemed necessary for maintaining existing social conditions.

In Western capitalism the prevailing ideological concepts include culturally conditioned ideas of freedom, individuality, national chauvinism, and the right to private ownership. The educational ISA systematically embeds the social hierarchy necessary for replicating such concepts. It does this through organizing its apprentices, as well as its dropouts and those that never even attended, towards the goal of maintaining the (minimum) two class divide of capitalist society, propelling the current mode of production.

The academic library as educational ISA, as a result, is in a plum position for assisting the college or university's ideologically driven, conservative goal of reproducing society in its familiar form, capitalism. But, besides being an educational ISA, the academic library is arguably a communications ISA (particularly because of its role as a vehicle for scholarly communication), a cultural ISA, and, as presented in the previous section, a religious ISA. As a religious ISA, or at least as an institution containing residual religious ideologies in the sense defined by Raymond Williams, the academic library is not only a manifestation of the currently dominant educational ISA, but a means of persistence for what Althusser identified as the previously dominant ISA, "the Church" (2001, 101).[2]

Gregory J. Levine argued that the survival of older ideologies under capitalism suggests that these stubborn institutions are retained because they profit capitalism (1986, 436). According to Eugen Schoenfeld, "submissive" religions with "other-worldly orientations," typified by the Abrahamic religions that are prominent in the West, are "by their very nature committed to obedience," and thus committed to the aims of the dominant class (1992, 116). Sociologist of religion Thomas Luckmann wrote that the "sacred cosmos permeates the various, or less clearly differentiated, institutional areas such as kinship, the division of labor and the regulation of the exercise of power" and that, as societies develop, specialized institutions emerge to regulate religion, and these institutions reflect the cosmic worldview of the society in which they operate (1970, 61-2). Considering the long history of institutional forms of religion, as well as religion's ability to stubbornly attach itself to ISAs and RSAs, it is reasonable to conclude that religious superstructures tend to be historically, politically, and culturally tenacious, as well as effective tools for propping up the *status quo*.

Capitalism is, by nature, hierarchical; it has to be in order to effectively coordinate production and squeeze maximum surplus value out of workers (Screpanti 1999, 5-6). Capitalism is also patriarchal; Friedrich Engels saw seeds of class division in the patriarchal family unit (1978,

---

2   For the purpose of this essay, I consider "the Church" to include both Catholic and the mainline Protestant Churches, as they both tend to represent the predominant religious currents in Western society, and both are characterized as patriarchal and hierarchical.

131), and the three major Abrahamic religions, Judaism, Christianity, and Islam, have, throughout history, effectively reflected, reinforced, and expanded this paternalism beyond the family to larger social groups.

Prior to capitalism, the Western religious ISA was embodied by the Church (Althusser 2001, 101): a particularly sturdy hierarchical and patriarchal religious ideology. The Church incorporated elements of the cultural and educational ISAs (102), and at times, various functions of the RSAs (as evidenced by the Inquisition). In the Medieval Church, the church building "was seen as a symbolic code: a 'model' of the cosmos and image of the Celestial City, imbued with divine order and harmony as were the heavenly spheres" (Schulenburg 2005, 185-6). In other words, the building and the people in it reflected the patriarchal and hierarchical nature of spiritual and ultimate reality and served as a template for ordering society as a whole. As a crypto-temple, the modern academic library, while not possessing the overt authority of the pre-capitalism era Church, retains certain elements, even if they might be somewhat enervated, of that institution's "symbolic code." The academic library is patriarchal in structure (Murgai 1991), and imposes a hierarchy upon itself and its inhabitants that is compatible with and allied to the capitalism in which it has survived.

The religious requirements of the crypto-temple, at least in the modern world, are implicit. Few if any people literally profess their religious faith to the academic library. Few if any people literally believe that an objective god or gods manifests in the library. It is not implausible, however, to see the crypto-temple as making ideological demands on those who enter its space, and it is reasonable to assume that these demands (1) reinforce a hierarchical and patriarchal schema in the service of the educational ISA, and are therefore, (2) in the service of the dominant classes.

The Library Subject's Interpellation as Supplicant

Those who enter the "sacred library" orient themselves in relationship to it. This happens, I suggest, when the library *qua* crypto-temple invites an ideological response and disposition in the individual. This response is both symptomatic of the capitalist mode of production and appropriate to that mode of production.

Maxwell eloquently encapsulated the religious presence of the academic library and the ways in which patrons acknowledge this presence:

> Others may be praying by simply coming to the library, for just being there may infuse them with the Force. Energy, vibrations, spirit, and life force point to this indescribable essence that seems palpable, especially when standing in one of the great reading rooms of a historic library building. Simply standing quietly amid the grandeur can be an act of devotion. As an awed second grader said upon entering such a massive library reading room, "God lives here." (2006, 17)

This feeling certainly does exist; I have experienced it myself while in academic libraries. It is perfectly reasonable for someone entering Harvard's Widener Library reading room to experience a sense of religious awe and cosmic insignificance when viewing its pillared entrance, cathedral-like space, and vaulted ceilings. Maxwell's quotation also suggests that the library patron, through her "devotion," accepts the "greater purpose" of the library, i.e., the sacred role of the library in (an ultimately historically conditioned and located) society. Assuming that the library is operating in its capacity as a religious ISA, this religious presence may be read as an ideological cue and the student's devotion as one way by which the ideology constitutes, or "interpellates" her.

For Althusser, "man is an ideological animal by nature" (2001, 116). People are ensnared within the ideological landscape through which they navigate. The religious experience of Maxwell's second grader indicates that the child has been interpellated. That is, her subjective experience has been configured by the latticework of ideologies that comprise her social milieu. Consciously or not, by being awed by the library she has acted appropriately in relation to the ideology of the library and has entered into the library's hierarchical space.

According to Althusser, interpellation is the process by which ideology constitutes the individual as a subject. Ideology does this by "calling out" to the individual, "hailing" her as a subject (2001, 118). Our second grader is both created as a subject by the ideology and subjected to the demands and "realities" of the ideology. That is, she recognizes and becomes *who she is* in terms of the ideological concepts imposed upon her by the institution. The second grader is a product of the web of relations; more precisely, *she is the web of relations* that arises from her encounter with the ideological symbols of the library. Ideology sets the subject's place at the table, the subject finds her seat, and the ISAs drive this interpellation.

As a religious ISA that reflects a patriarchal and hierarchical worldview and acts as the henchman of the educational ISA, the modern academic library as crypto-temple explicitly and implicitly determines the range of behaviors and potential actions patrons may perform in its spaces. If a patron fits the proper ideological profile, obeys the rules, performs the rituals, and acts out her ideological part, she is rewarded with access to knowledge/the holy and helped to secure her place in the cosmos "sanctified" by the library:

> If [the subject] believes in Duty, he will have the corresponding attitudes, inscribed in ritual practices 'according to the correct principles'. If he believes in justice, he will submit unconditionally to the rules of the Law, and may even protest when they are violated, sign petitions, take part in a demonstration, etc. (Althusser 2001, 113)

If the subject acknowledges, consciously or implicitly, the "sacredness" of the crypto-temple—in actuality a skein of religious symbolism masking the reified social relations of capitalism—she accepts the socially accepted narratives concerning the academic library in the society in which she exists and acts accordingly within its walls, while at the same time being conditioned to be a part of that larger society.

Adopting Althusser's concept of ideology in order to make a preliminary attempt at parsing the ways in which academic libraries as crypto-temples utilize ideology, I suggest that there is a continuum, bounded by two primary modes of expression, which is useful to describe the library patron's interpellation:

- The library patron interpellates as a religious *disenfranchisee* on the periphery or outside of the ISA, helping to maintain the *status quo* through reproducing existing class structures.

- The library patron interpellates as an *initiate* inside the ISA, integrating into the hierarchy of the library, presenting no challenge to the *status quo*, and helping to reproduce class division in an information-driven society.

At the bottom of the ideological continuum are the "unbaptized," the "unclean," the *disenfranchisees*. These are those individuals who are excluded from the library or have only limited access to it because of the particular library's—similar to many churches—charitable mandate. Non-affiliated community users often wear this mantle. They enjoy the least access of those with access; they may feel "out of place" when using the library, or they may think that they cannot or should not use it because of feelings that they "don't belong." They often appear incongruous in the sacred spaces of the library frequented by *initiates*, and, to be honest, they are sometimes treated as the "other" when encountered in these spaces by library staff and institutionally affiliated patrons.

Besides these lower echelon users of the library, there are those *disenfranchisees* that have been excluded because they have refused or vitiated the necessary rituals of the library; they are meted out appropriate punishment according to the ISA's ideological framework. For example, people that flout the library's often unwritten call for silence risk temporary or permanent "excommunication" through exclusion. Another example: some instructors mistakenly conclude that legitimate knowledge exists only under the aegis of the library as a "sanctified" institution, and may penalize students that rely upon resources that they have obtained through other channels. Finally, there are those self-selectors that fully or partially exclude themselves from library services because of library anxiety (Mellon 1986).

In rejecting the sacred in its institutional capacity, one rejects its protections and largesse, and therefore may be seen as rebelling against the "natural" order of the larger society which the library appears to engrave with religious structure and symbolism. The offending patron is rightly corrected according to the ideology of the Church/crypto-temple. The library excommunicant, whether formally (legally) excluded or a self-selected exile, suffers a very religious punishment; she is left to make her way through the chaos of profane information space as one of the unenlightened. Again, this is natural for capitalism, which relies upon hierarchical arrangement, and therefore relies upon the existence of the excluded.[3]

---

3   Marx described capitalism's necessity for surplus population in *Capital* (781-94).

As we move up the hierarchy of library users, we observe a range of institutionally affiliated users (e.g., undergraduates, graduate students, and faculty members); the "legitimate" patrons, the *initiates*. Level of access and confidence in navigating the sacred library varies according to the social position of the patron within the academic community. These also depend on how much the *initiate* "gets it," that is, the degree to which she acknowledges the power of the library as paradigmatic of her larger society and understands how to approach and work with this power. This hierarchy peaks ultimately with the librarians, the secular priests that have the most complete entrée to the Holy of Holies, and who regulate patrons' access, sometimes doing so in accordance with these patrons' status in the hierarchy.

The *initiate* is comfortable (enough) interacting with the hierarchical religious symbolism of the academic library to use it at various levels of effectiveness. As a legitimized and hierarchically oriented patron of the library, she accepts as natural the hierarchical ordering of the library as well as the universe that is a reflection of her "cosmic mountain." The *initiate* is capable of integrating within this hierarchy in order to "play the game." That is, she engages in the necessary rituals and observances required to operate legally within the ISA, to maintain her status in the ISA, to cement her conceptions and status in the ideological universe illuminated by the library as ISA, and to help ensure the ideology's persistence as an ISA and therefore as one engine for replicating the capitalist social hierarchy.

When functioning correctly as an ISA, the academic library acts as a stepladder for restocking capitalism's "middle class technicians, white-collar workers, small and middle executives, [and] petty bourgeois of all kinds" (Althusser 2001, 105). It does this largely because it enshrines the educational ISA's ideological imperatives in an institution that impresses these imperatives as cosmic structure.[4] The *initiate* invests in the "greater purpose," of the library. The pursuit of knowledge, however, becomes hopelessly imbedded with the capitalist structural hierarchy taught by the library and exhibited by its religious symbolism.

---

4   Other elements of the educational ISA may also function to replicate this cosmic structure, but the academic library's role as crypto-temple makes it particularly apparent.

CALL TO ACTION

Librarians actively support concepts such as democracy, equality, and the free-flow of information (American Library Association 2010, 49), even though they work in institutions that incorporate residual yet powerful ideological structures that support the exploitative tendencies of modern capitalism. In the West, the academic library's hierarchical structure, true to its roots in the Church, determines the level of access one has to its knowledge/religious mysteries, and this level of access plays a role in determining the patron's subsequent incorporation into society. The patriarchal hierarchies of the academic library as crypto-church serves as a useful framework for taking the ideology of the paternal family unit and abstracting it to subsume the main classes found in capitalism. It then conditions members of these classes, even if subtly, in a tried and true ideological environment, a crypto-religious environment that has proven itself amenable to capitalism.

I noted at the beginning of this essay that, through most of history, libraries were also temples, and that they very often served to maintain the political/economic *status quo*. This appears to remain the case with modern academic libraries despite that the religious elements have become submerged in the library's structure. These elements are, however, in need of further excavation and illumination.

It has been my intent for this essay to be prefatory; additional work must be done. Further research should tease out the relationships between the library's religious symbolisms and the prerogatives of the library in its capacity as educational ISA, as well as the other ISAs active in the library as an institution (that is, the communications ISA, the cultural ISA, and possibly the political ISA). Researchers should also focus on further understanding how these symbolisms mold library patrons' actions related to library use or non-use.

Finally, both researchers and practitioners should investigate and develop interventions to counteract effects of the library as temple. That is, they should explore ways to desacralize the library, to make the knowledge environment more participatory and less stratified (such as by championing the Open Access movement), to make more transparent the societal relations embodied by the academic library through praxis, and to work to shift the library's ideological footprint towards emergent and equitable counterhegemonic ideologies.

Works Cited

Althusser, Louis. 2005. *For Marx.* Translated by Ben Brewster. London: Verso.

—-. 2001. *Lenin and Philosophy and Other Essays.* Translated by Ben Brewster. New York: Monthly Review Press.

American Library Association. 2010. *Intellectual Freedom Manual.* 8th ed. Chicago: American Library Association.

Arksey, Laura. 1977. "The Library of Assurbanipal, King of the World." *Wilson Library Bulletin* 51: 833-840.

Benton Foundation. 1997. "Buildings, Books, and Bytes: Libraries and Communities in the Digital Age." *Library Trends* 46 (1): 178-223.

Brown, Michelle P. 2007. "The Book as Sacred Space." In *Sacred Space: House of God, Gate of Heaven*, edited by Philip North and John North, 43-63. London, Continuum.

Buchanan, Dennis. 1986. "Ancient Greek Libraries." *State Librarian* 34 (3): 40-42.

Callinicos, Alex. 1976. *Althusser's Marxism.* London: Pluto Press.

Cole, John Y. 1979. "Storehouses and Workshops: American Libraries and the Uses of Knowledge." In *The Organization of Knowledge in Modern America, 1860-1920*, edited by Alexandra Oleson and John Voss, 364-85. Baltimore, MD: John Hopkins University Press.

Cupitt, Don. 1984. *The Sea of Faith.* London: Cambridge University.

De Vleeschauwer, H. J. 1963. *History of the Western Library.* Pretoria: Pretoria University.

—-. "Afterword." 1977. In *The Oral Antecedents of Greek Librarianship*, by H. Curtis Wright. Provo, UT: Brigham Young University Press.

Eliade, Mircea. 1987. *The Sacred and the Profane: The Nature of Religion*, translated by Willard R. Trask. San Diego: Harcourt.

Elliott, Gregory. 1993. "The Lonely Hour of the Last Instance: Louis Pierre Althusser, 1918-1990." In *The Althusserian Legacy*, edited by E. Ann Kaplan and Michael Sprinker, 233-39. London: Verso.

Engels, Frederick. 1978. *The Origin of the Family, Private Property and the State*, translated by Alec West. New York: International Publishers.

Erskine, Andrew. 1995. "Culture and Power in Ptolemaic Egypt: The Museum and Library of Alexandria." *Greece and Rome* 42 (1): 38-48.

Gorman, Michael. 2000. *Our Enduring Values: Librarianship in the 21ˢᵗ Century*. Chicago: American Library Association.

Gramsci, Antonio. 1978. *Selections from the Prison Notebooks*, translated and edited by Quinton Hoare and Geoffrey Nowell Smith. New York: International Publishers.

Harris, Michael H. 1986. "State, Class, and Cultural Reproduction: Toward a Theory of Library Service in the United States." In *Advances in Librarianship*, edited by Wesley Simonton, 14:21-252. Orlando, FL: Academic Press.

—-. 1995. *History of the Libraries in the Western World*. 4ᵗʰ ed. Metuchen, NJ.

Hessel, Alfred. 1950. *A History of Libraries*, translated by Reuben Peiss. Washington, DC: Scarecrow Press.

Jackson, Sidney L. 1974. *Libraries and Librarianship in the West: A Brief History*. New York: McGraw-Hill.

Knipe, David M. 1988. "The Temple in Image and Reality." In *Temple and Society*, edited by Michael V. Fox. Winona Lake, IN: Eisenbrauns.

Levine, Gregory J. 1986. "On the Geography of Religion." *Transactions of the Institute of British Geographers, New Series* 11 (4): 428-440.

Luckmann, Thomas. 1970. *The Invisible Religion*. London: Macmillan.

Marx, Karl. 1990. *Capital: A Critique of Political Economy, Volume 1*. Translated by Ben Fowkes. London: Penguin Books.

—-. 1992. *Early Writings*. Translated by Rodney Livingstone and Gregor Benton. Chippenham, Wiltshire: Penguin Books.

Marx, Karl, and Friedrich Engels. 1998. *The German Ideology*. Amherst, NY: Prometheus Books.

Maxwell, Nancy Kalikow. 2006. *Sacred Stacks: the Higher Purpose of Libraries and Librarianship*. Chicago, American Library Association.

Mellon, Constance. 1986. "Library Anxiety: A Grounded Theory and Its Development," *College & Research Libraries* 47 (2): 160-165.

Murgai, Sarla R. 1991. "Attitudes Toward Women as Managers in Library and Information Science." *Sex Roles* 24 (11/12): 681-699.

Newell, William Lloyd. 1986. *The Secular Magi: Marx, Freud, and Nietzche on Religion*. New York: Pilgrim Press.

Oppenheim, A. Leo. 1964. *Ancient Mesopotamia: Portrait of a Dead Civilization*. Chicago: University of Chicago Press.

—-. 1960. "Assyriology—Why and How?" *Current Anthropology* 1 (5-6): 409-423.

Parsons, Edward Alexander. 1952. *Alexandrian Library: Glory of the Hellenic World; Its Rise, Antiquities, and Destructions*. Amsterdam: Elsevier.

Raber, Douglas. 2003. "Librarians as Organic Intellectuals: A Gramscian Approach to Blind Spots and Tunnel Vision." *Library Quarterly* 73 (1): 33-53.

Raines, John, ed. 2002. "Introduction." In *Marx on Religion*, by Karl Marx. Philadelphia: Temple University Press.

Schulenburg, Jane Tibbetts. 2005. "Gender, Celibacy, and Proscriptions of Sacred Space: Symbol and Practice." In *Women's Space: Patronage, Place, and Gender in the Medieval Church*, edited by Virginia Chieffo Raguin and Sarah Stanbury. Albany, NY: State University of New York Press.

Schoenfeld, Eugen. 1992. "Militant and Submissive Religions: Class, Religion and Ideology." *The British Journal of Sociology* 43 (1): 111-140.

Screpanti, Ernesto. 1999. "Capitalist Forms and the Essence of Capitalism." *Review of International Political Economy* 6 (1): 1-26.

Sung, Jung Mo. 2011. *The Subject, Capitalism, and Religion*. New York: Palgrave Macmillan.

Thompson, James Westfall. 1962. *Ancient Libraries*. Hamden, CT: Archon Books.

Wente, Edward F. 1995. "Scribes of Ancient Egypt." In *Civilizations of the Ancient Near East*, 4 vols., edited by Jack M. Sasson, 2211-21 New York: Charles Scribner's Sons.

Williams, Raymond. 2009. *Marxism and Literature*. Oxford: Oxford University Press.

Social Reproduction in the Early American Public Library: Exploring the Connections between Capital and Gender[1]

Alexandra Carruthers

> The library, in its influence, is whatever the librarian makes it; it seems destined to become an all-pervading force ... moulding public opinion, educating to all the higher possibilities of human thought and action; to become a means for enriching, beautifying, and making fruitful the barren places in human life ... Librarians have an important part to play in the history of civilization and in the conservation of the race.
>
> *Linda A. Eastman*

Eastman's enthusiastic vision of the social role of libraries, published in *Library Journal* in 1897 weaves together the topics of this paper: the influence of industrial capitalism and the increasingly female workforce with the public library movement and its ambitious goals (80). At first, and most evidently, it demonstrates the idealism of early public librarians who believed that the public library brought the

1   I want to thank Dr. Toni Samek, Dr. Brent Ryan Bellamy and Diana Wilson for their assistance reviewing this work. I'd also like to thank Dr. Sioban Stevenson for her excellent dissertation which provided an incredibly useful source of both inspiration and historical information.

United States a great deal closer to perfecting its great experiment in democracy. Wrapped up in the trope of Eastman's fertility metaphor is the presence of women librarians, a growing population of mostly single, white, middle-class, educated women whose allegedly innate womanly abilities to nurture and cultivate man's moral and cultural sensitivities were directed away from the individual family unit and towards the service of the whole people. Finally, in her expansive view of the history of civilization and the conservation of humanity, Eastman anticipates the tenor of millionaire industry captain and philanthropist Andrew Carnegie. In his *Gospel of Wealth* (1889) Carnegie argues that the competition of the marketplace is necessary for the progress of civilization, for though it produces class disparity, it places wealth in the hands of great men capable of distributing it in the service of the common good "and the elevation of our race" (12). Like Eastman, the institution Carnegie was increasingly ideologically and materially invested in as a force for the common good was the public library. This paper attempts to unravel and set in clearer relation these three threads: the public library movement, the increasingly female labour force within that movement and the economic context of industrial capitalism that was shaping them both.

Eastman's words were published during a period when librarianship in the United States was undergoing radical transformations. From 1875 to 1926 the number of libraries open and free to the public grew from 342 to 5,954 (Valentine 2005, 48). The construction of these public libraries was funded by philanthropists or local associations, usually women's clubs, and then they were handed over to municipalities to be supported through taxation. Carnegie donated the funds for 1,679 library buildings in the United States and thousands more internationally between 1881 and 1920 (Stauffer 2006, 3). The demographic shift within the profession from predominantly men to predominantly women in this period was similarly dramatic. According to the United States census, women comprised 20% of all librarians in 1870 (Schiller 1974, 125), but by 1920 they comprised 88% of librarians (Maack 1998, 52). Indeed, the appearance in this period of the occupation's "allegedly feminine traits" is attributed to this demographic shift (Schiller 1974, 123). Not surprisingly, the social role of the public library and women's ability to contribute to that role were a topic for regular discussion in librarianship's professional literature of the period.[2]

Library historians have attempted to understand the feminization of librarianship in relation to its historical context and the public library movement[3] and in relation to the profession—its character, professional status and inequitable pay and power structures.[4] As most of this writing comes out of the feminist movement, there appears to be consensus that femininity, as it was performed at the time, was culturally constructed. However, there has been no investigation into how the ideological and material forces that shaped the late nineteenth-century concept of white middle-class femininity can be seen to influence the public library movement. To address this gap in research and elucidate such a complex period in U.S. history, this paper takes up the Marxist feminist concept of social reproduction, which articulates the relationship between industrial production and so-called "women's work." That the early public library was established in the service of reproducing the values of the capitalist ruling class has been argued extensively;[5] however, these arguments do not address the concurrent feminization of librarianship.

Marxist feminist theorists such as Selma James, Mariarosa Dalla Costa and Maya Andrea Gonzalez argue that women's unpaid labour in the home, (feeding, clothing and caring for their husbands, children, and themselves), while it is masked as biological destiny, serves to reproduce the labour power that is exploited by the

---

2 Weibel and Heim (1979) have usefully collected primary examples of this professional discussion in *The Role of Women in Librarianship, 1876 – 1976: the Entry, Advancement, and Struggle for Equalization in One Profession*. See also Dewey "Notes from 'Librarianship as a Profession for College-Bred Women.'"

3 *See* Schiller; Van Slyck; Maack; Valentine; and Stauffer

4 *See* Garrison; Weibel & Heim; and R. Harris

5 *See* Harris 68; Pawley 137; and Stevenson 27-69; similar critiques of large philanthropic efforts appear across the social sciences. In the Introduction to the interdisciplinary collection *Philanthropy and Cultural Imperialism* (1980), Robert F. Arnove writes "foundations like Carnegie, Rockefeller, and Ford ... represent relatively unregulated and unaccountable concentrations of power and wealth which buy talent, promote causes, and, in effect, establish an agenda of what merit's society's attention. They serve as "cooling-out" agencies, delaying and preventing more radical, structural change. They help maintain an economic and political order, international in scope, which benefits the ruling-class interests of philanthropists ... a system which ... has worked against the interests of minorities, the working class, and Third World peoples" (1).

capitalist. Indeed, without a fed, clothed and socialized workforce, there would be no workforce. The term *social reproduction* refers to women's domestic labour, which appears external to capitalist production but is actually constitutive of it. This paper will illustrate how capital's need for the social reproduction of labour power influenced both how femininity and women's work were defined and what public libraries were established to achieve. Tracing these ideologies through historical sources sheds light on evidence that women were actively recruited to librarianship for their feminine qualities: femininity was recognized as an existing solution to the problem of social unrest that public libraries aspired to solve. Though many public librarians were ostensibly, and sincerely, working in the interest of promoting social mobility for the working classes, public librarianship's embrace of femininity as a socially reproductive force helped to re-inscribe existing structural relationships between the classes and the genders.

American historian Gerda Lerner clearly articulates the materialist and feminist premises on which this research is founded in her introduction to *The Creation of Patriarchy* (1986). Lerner explains that when she approaches history she begins with "the assumption that men and women are biologically different, but that the values and implications based on that difference are the result of culture" (6). She also begins with the conviction "that patriarchy as a system is historical: it has a beginning in history. If that is so, it can be ended by historical process" (6). She argues that while women have not had the power to interpret and give significance to their own history, women "are and always have been actors and agents in history" (4). As such, her mission as a historian is to bring us closer to a vision of "the true-relations of the whole" (12). Going farther than "compensatory history," which simply adds women into the framework of history established by patriarchy, Lerner aspires to make the vision of women equal to the vision of men (12). Producing scholarship on the history of women works towards this goal because "the relation of men and women to the knowledge of their past is in itself a shaping force in the making of history" (7). Guiding Lerner's research is the question "What is the relationship of ideas, and specifically of ideas about gender, to the social and economic forces that shape history?" (10). This paper's guiding question, "What is the relationship of ideas about gender to the social and economic forces that shaped early public librarianship?" is directly influenced by Lerner's work.[6]

HISTORICAL CONTEXT

Melvil Dewey dated the modern library movement to August 1876 with the establishment of the American Library Association (ALA). This was the American Gilded Age (1870s-1890s), and the movement continued to grow into the Progressive Era (1890s-1920s). These were both periods of rapid change: women were challenging the boundaries of their domestic sphere of influence, the working class was struggling against the yoke of industrial capitalism, and Progressive political reform was expanding government services that they hoped would guide the changing nation towards harmony and prosperity (Hildenbrand 1985, 185-6). This section elaborates on the ideological tensions between capital and labour coming to a head in this time, particularly through the lens of the Knights of Labour union, and on the women's movement, as these two contexts formed the backdrop and motivation for the public library movement and the feminization of the profession.

The expansion of women's influence and the public library movement were both responses to the social and economic upheaval of the end of the nineteenth century and beginning of the twentieth. The landscape of the Northeastern and Midwestern United States was dramatically transforming. Education historians Samuel Bowles and Herbert Gintis explain that there was rapid urbanization, and "the growth of wage employment, the increasing similarity among workers in the conditions of employment, and the hardship of three major depressions in the course of two decades spurred the development

---

6   This chapter is necessarily narrower in scope than Lerner's book. The ideas about gender discussed are primarily those experienced by late nineteenth century white middle class women. Broad claims about femininity are founded on Sylvia Federici's claim that "if 'femininity' has been constituted in capitalist society as a work-function masking the production of the work-force under the cover of biological destiny, then 'women's history' is 'class history'" (2004, 14). Though, the topic and research of this paper could be expanded and nuanced by more attention to how race and class modified conceptions and experiences of femininity. Likewise, the geographic scope of this paper centers around the Northeastern and Midwestern United States as these were the seats of American industrialization, the women's movement, and the public library movement.

of organized resistance" (2011, 183). In 1894, labour journalist John Swinton reported "nine percent of the population owned eighty-four percent of the wealth, while ninety-one percent were in straightened circumstances, living from hand to mouth" (31). A vibrant labour community actively undermined capitalist ideology and worked towards improving the conditions of all workers; while, Carnegie, in the interest of capital, identified working class ideology as a threat and began investing in public libraries, an institution that had the potential to help workers see the errors of their ways.

The labour movement in the 1880s provided a powerful alternative to capitalist ideology that posed a serious threat to capital's power –though, by the turn of the century, it had lost some of its strength. Sioban Stevenson writes that "at no other time before or since [the 1880s] was the social identity of labour as powerful, or the hegemonic project of capital so vulnerable" (2005, 29). She uses the Knights of Labor (KoL) union to exemplify the force competing against capital for control of the means of production. The KoL were the "captains of America's labor movement" and "their membership was open to all workers: skilled, unskilled, women, immigrants, and even those sections of the middle class sympathetic to the cause" (35). More than demanding recompense for a set of grievances, the KoL's critique of unregulated industrial capitalism "extended to all aspects of life: economic, social, cultural and ... political" (36). Furthermore, the KoL proposed not just an alternate ideology but alternative practices; as David Scobey writes, the KoL "would pose alternative productive relations to the marketplace, an alternative conception of the republican polity, even an alternative morality to this 'present system of all for self'" (1984, 292). In 1892, the Carnegie Steel Company (CSC) defeated the KoL and the the Amalgamated Association of Iron and Steel Workers at the infamous and bloody Homestead strike. After refusing to negotiate on a reduction in wages, the CSC employed tactics such as a lock out, evicting workers from company-owned homes, and bringing in Pinkerton guards and state militia to suppress worker actions. Three Pinkerton agents and seven workers were killed and 40 workers were variously charged with murder, conspiracy, aggravated rioting and treason (Stevenson 2005, 32). With the full strength of capital and the state brought down against their efforts, the strength of the KoL began to wane.

Stevenson points out that though organized labour was critical of Carnegie's library philanthropy,[7] they believed in the importance of an educated populace and created their own libraries to support their members. At the peak of the KoL's influence, public libraries funded by philanthropists and women's clubs and maintained by municipal governments were not the only source of library resources for the working class. The differing structure of the KoL's libraries and public libraries reflected the differing ideologies that motivated them: "while Carnegie emphasized independent study, labour appeared to encourage a more social approach to knowledge acquisition" (2005, 42). Carnegie's conceptualization of libraries as spaces for isolated study reflected the individualism central to his personal philosophy of Social Darwinism. In contrast, KoL libraries strove to balance independent study with collective learning practices such as debate and discussion. The Homestead strike was a defeat, at the time, of an ideology of library service that emphasized collective over individual improvement.

As the nation industrialized, the feminine domestic sphere was set in contrast to the masculine public sphere, and the allegedly natural qualities and skills of womanhood were believed to serve a particular social purpose. Harriet Sigerman explains that

> [m]arried women were expected to be nurturing, maternal wives and mothers. The harsh realm of business and manufacture drove men and women to view the home as a sanctuary, a place in which the values of love, harmony and virtue reigned... This role invested women with special power and influence. (2000, 239)

As Dee Garrison puts it, "It would be almost impossible to overemphasize the Victorian conviction that men were physically tamed and morally elevated by the sway of the gentle female" (1979, 177). Women, though relegated to a position of financial dependence were not conceived of as entirely passive creatures. Women's role was to actively create a space that embodied and made possible the virtues

---

7   *See* Robert Martin's *Carnegie Denied: Communities Rejecting Carnegie Library Construction Grant*. This work provides a history of the communities, primarily communities sympathetic to the labour movement, that rejected Carnegie's philanthropy.

of love and harmony. They were also responsible for morally shaping their children and husbands. Furthermore, though women had no political rights of their own, they were "obligated to raise liberty-loving sons" and they "dutifully discharged these tasks of citizenship" (Sigerman 2000, 206). This ideal of "Republican Motherhood," in fact, was an early justification for women's literacy and education (Malone 1996, 280). Despite the disparity of circumstance across class and racial lines, the public widely accepted womanly virtues and their embodiment in the home to be biologically determined.[8]

Women's domestic responsibilities outside the home also expanded in the late nineteenth century. Following the civil war, the "need for more teachers and for women who were able to step into positions left vacant by men lost in war" motivated the opening of college education to white women and the great influx of women students, particularly in the north (Sigerman 2000, 313). Throughout this period, the universal suffrage movement continued and gained acceptance—eventually winning women the vote in 1920. Middle class white women also emerged as forces in the public sphere through the women's club movement and the temperance movement.

Rather than rejecting the notion that the domestic sphere was women's rightful place, the women's movement expanded the concept of the domestic sphere and emphasized its importance. It was women's insistence on the power of essential womanly virtues, which alone could temper the harsh male-dominated public sphere that grounded women's claims to authority and relevance. Frances Willard, president of the Women's Christian Temperance Union, declared in 1884 that the purpose of her organization "[was] to make the whole world *homelike*" (quoted in Sigerman 2000, 342). Women leaders of this time worked against the odds to address social inequality and make a meaningful difference in the lives of many. But their efforts were notably limited by their commitment to reproducing white middle-class values (Olsen & Ritchie 2006, xv).

---

8   As an example of how wide-spread and established the given concept of femininity was, Garrison quotes an 1875 ruling of the Wisconsin Supreme Court, which declared "The law of nature destines and qualifies the female sex for the bearing and nurturing of the children of our race and for the custody of the homes of the world" (1979, 173).

Femininity—its Expression and Function

The feminization of a profession refers not only to a demographic change in a profession but also to the profession's adoption of feminine characteristics (Schiller 1974, 123). Histories offered by Garrison, Mary Niles Maack and Abigail A. Van Slyck say that librarianship took on feminine characteristics as the field became demographically dominated by women, in other words, women brought their feminine characteristics with them to the profession. Garrison argues that the feminization of librarianship transformed the librarian's role into that of a "genteel library hostess" (1979, 179). She writes, "the librarian stood "always ready to serve," to anticipate wants, and to do "the honors of a library as a hostess"" (179). In Garrison's view, women librarians' submissiveness contributed to the profession's precariously funded semi-professional status. More recently, Maack attributes some of public libraries' most noble qualities to the influence of women. She writes, "[women] brought to the field a gender-linked value system that emphasized altruism, advocacy, and intellectual nurturing of children and adults" (1998, 51). Van Slyck agrees that women brought progressive values with them to the profession, and she argues that through their experimentation with their new professional roles women librarians caused Carnegie libraries to "take on roles and meanings that had been unintended by the benefactor" (1995, 161). These three critiques focus on the influence of women after the demographic shift, but spend little time considering its initial cause.

Schiller disagrees that it was women themselves who imposed feminine qualities on the profession from their positions in the lower levels of the bureaucratic hierarchy. Schiller suggests instead that the recruitment of women into library education by male library leaders was a major factor in the feminization of librarianship and that male leaders appealed to women by identifying their "allegedly natural suitability for library work" (1974, 126). Library leaders were motivated to represent librarianship as feminine, she argues, in order to fill low-paying positions that required educated workers. The growing number of female college graduates satisfied these requirements. She admits however that feminization was "most likely a two-way process, spurred and reinforced by broader socioeconomic and cultural forces" (130). Schiller dismisses women's "allegedly natural suitability" for library work as a motivating factor in their recruitment by library leaders too quickly. With only slight modification, Schiller's argument gathers a fuller explanatory power: library leaders were motivated to recruit women into librarianship not just for their cheap labour, but also because the emerging social goal of the public library was to fill a traditionally feminine role. From an economic perspective, women's work was to socially reproduce the workforce on the level of the family – the function of the public library was to socially reproduce the workforce on an institutional level. Drawing a connection between the ideals of femininity and the economic function of women's work reveals how thoroughly capitalist ideology motivated the feminization of librarianship.

Marxist feminist theorists identify an economic purpose behind the development of the domestic sphere and women's work. Distinct from economic relationships under earlier modes of production, like slavery or feudal vassalage, workers under capitalism are responsible for their own upkeep. Gonzalez writes, "If wages are too low, or if their services are no longer needed, workers are free to survive by other means (as long as those means are legal). The reproduction of the workers is thus emphatically not the responsibility of the capitalist" (2011, 227). However, in *Capital Volume I* (1867), Karl Marx explains that for an industry to be productive and profitable it must consume labour power. Capital provides a wage to workers in exchange for the only commodity they are able to sell, their labour. For their labour, workers are given pay "that is enough to live on (more or less) and to reproduce other workers" (James 1972, 11). Marxist feminism points out that there is another side to the wage relation that Marx does not describe in detail, and that is how labour power itself is originally produced. James explains that in order for a labourer to exist he must be born and cared for; in other words, "To describe [the labourer's] basic production and reproduction is to describe women's work" (11). The division of labour into a private, domestic, female sphere and a public, male sphere is thus central to the wage relation under capital. From a Marxist feminist perspective, the rigid definition of femininity, motherhood and women's work under late nineteenth-century American industrial capitalism can be understood as symptomatic of these underlying economic relations.

The work of social reproduction includes not only the physical reproduction of labourers, but also the reproduction of social values and norms. In the late nineteenth century, this work—discipline, childbearing and caring for a family—was considered women's work. James and Dalla Costa explain that women "on the one hand discipline the children who will be workers tomorrow and on the other hand discipline the husband to work today, for only his wage can pay for labor power to be reproduced" (1972, 48). The idealized woman of the late nineteenth century was anything but a disciplinarian, but the promotion of morality was one of her key social roles. In an article that explains how institutions, such as libraries and library schools, can exert a cultural influence that supports the interests of the ruling class, Christine Pawley writes that the hegemonic power of the dominant class can be maintained consensually rather than coercively, "when it gains control over a range of values and norms, to the extent that these are so embedded in society that they receive unquestioned acceptance" (1998, 127). As it was tied to the biological expression of her gender, women's moral influence was widely respected and the interests that their moral influence served were left unquestioned. The social influence it was women's role to exert fits precisely the needs of the early public library, as is particularly clear in Carnegie's own introduction of the public library and its benefits to his own workforce.

Carnegie's Rhetoric and Social Reproduction

A close reading of Carnegie's speech, "The Common Interest of Labor and Capital: An Address to Working Men" also detects capital's need for the support of a separate sphere of social reproduction. Carnegie first gave this speech in 1889 at the opening of the new public library in Braddock, Pennsylvania and more or less repeated it at the openings of libraries in Pittsburg, Allegheny and Homestead (Stevenson 2005, 5). Here, Carnegie speaks from the standpoint of industrial capital and articulates its interests. His speech describes the ideal worker and identifies the library as a tool that will help his audience improve their conditions in life. The cause of the tension between capital and labour, he explains, is not wealth disparity or job insecurity, it is lack of education. For Carnegie, the ideal worker has a very specific education, which begins with "useful knowledge" (1968, 66). This education is first specialized to their field and then expanded to include a little of everything, particularly economics. In fact, in Carnegie's view, the library "will have justified its existence" if it assists the labourer in understanding "the economic laws which hold the capitalists in their relentless grasp" because this will "obviate most of the difficulties which arise between these two forces [labour and capital]" (70). Later in his speech Carnegie provides an example of the type of economic understanding he hopes the workers will gain by describing his own subjection to the law of competition. He explains that, even though he would like to, he cannot reduce the working day from 12 hours to eight because it would put the company at a competitive disadvantage (72). Carnegie's ideal worker, understanding that his working day was determined by immutable and unchallengeable economic laws, would resign himself to his work schedule, cease agitating with the union, and aspire to improve his individual conditions by moving up the company ranks.

In addition to being educated in his trade and in economics, the ideal worker is self-motivated, for as Carnegie argues, the man who fails to rise "has to find fault not in the firm, or the manager, or the foreman, but in himself" (1968, 72).[9] The industrialist explains to his audience that employers actively seek out men with exceptional abilities in order to promote them, and that workers should take inspiration from library books which are filled with stories of "the rise of many men from our own ranks" (71).[10] "The Library," he announces, "will give [working men] an opportunity to make themselves more valuable to their employers" (57). Put another way, Carnegie's speech makes clear that he funded libraries so that they would assist in the social reproduction of the type of ambitious worker that is the most valuable to their employers.

Creating and supporting (reproducing) the type of worker described above was necessary for Carnegie because the alternative, a worker who supported the union and demanded steady wages and an eight hour work day, threatened to disrupt production at his steel mills and undermine his company's competitive advantage. The worker who saw himself as an individual and worked outside of his

---

9   As a side note, Carnegie adds that an ideal worker is also able to relax and enjoy himself; providing himself as an example, Carnegie reveals that the secret to his own success is that "trouble runs off [his] back like water from a duck" (1968, 71).

10   Carnegie's use of "our" identifies himself with the working men. This is likely a reference to his well-publicized personal history—as Carnegie himself was born to a working class immigrant family.

12 hour shifts to improve his skills, distinguish himself from his co-workers and become upwardly mobile would not only be profitable to the company, but would also undermine the strength of the union, which depended on the solidarity of the workers. As if he were an egalitarian, Carnegie declares "[t]here is no man who may not rise to the highest position" (1968, 72). However, in this speech he abstains from mentioning his belief that "inequality of environment" is one of the "conditions to which we must accommodate ourselves" (1889, 5). Carnegie believed there was not room at the top for everyone. While he claims any individual man is capable of raising his socioeconomic position, Carnegie recognized that the competitive process of reaching the top necessarily leaves people below – thus, for him, inequality must exist of necessity. The library, for Carnegie, is not a tool meant to offer social mobility to everyone, but only to the individuals able to distinguish themselves from the rest. In contrast to the KoL's library, structured with the goal of improving quality of life for all, Carnegie's public libraries were meant to facilitate the occasional personal improvement in a system that remained structurally the same.

The work of socially reproducing middle class values, particularly the reproduction of Carnegie's ideal individualistic workers, was actively pursued by librarians in the period. Based on a survey of *Library Journal* and *Public Libraries* between 1880 and 1915, Stevenson concludes that when discussing services to labour or general management policy, library discourse conforms to and supports "capital's requirements with respect to the social relations of production" (2005, 52).[11] For example, the first issue of the journal *Public Libraries*, published in 1896, includes an extensive "Library Primer" written by then-president of the ALA, John Cotton Dana. This article promotes the development of new public libraries that fulfill Carnegie's library ideal. Dana writes, "A proper and worthy aim of the public library is the supplying of books on every profession, art, or handicraft, that workers in every department who care to study may perfect themselves in their work" (1896, 5). He continues,

---

11   Stevenson also finds that when discussing citizenship, public library discourse and the KoL's discourse share common language. Both agree that all citizens should be well educated, though professional literature betrays a fear of worker ignorance, while the KoL argue that intelligence, not wealth, should be grounds for citizenship (2005, 62).

The public library, then, is a means for elevating and refining the taste, for giving greater efficiency to every worker, for diffusing sound principles of social and political action, for furnishing intellectual culture to all, and is a powerful co-worker with the church in endeavoring to lead men to a higher life. (6)

Dana's is a noble sentiment, but in its historical context it represents a rejection of unionism and a whole-hearted acceptance of capital's values. The provision of skill-improving resources for workers who "care to study" reflects Dana's support for the competitive model of social mobility for the few over collective improvement. In his emphasis on worker efficiency Dana parrots Carnegie's exhortation that working men use the library to become more valuable to their employers. Finally, the innocuous appeal to "sound principles of social and political action" holds an implicit critique of social and political principles and action that are inconsistent with the competitive model he elevates, such as union tactics and ideology. This primer was published only four years after the deadly Homestead strike. Dana's vision of librarianship is of an institution that helps resolve problems of social unrest by supporting workers who desire to compete against their fellow workers for the limited prize of social mobility.

WOMEN'S WORK AND WOMEN LIBRARIANS

Librarians surveyed in 1903 considered women's "natural" skills and abilities, particularly those that softened and tempered disharmony, to be transferable to librarianship. In 1904 Salome Cutler Fairchild gave a report at the ALA conference on the status of women in librarianship based on this survey, which had been distributed to 100 libraries. She explains that in all of the responses "[i]t is quite generally conceded that in positions that do not involve the highest degree of executive or business ability but which require a certain 'gracious hospitality,' women as a class far surpass men" (1979, 54). She lists a number of positions in the library that women are suited to, including "all work with children" and then provides a summary of women's qualities that make them effective at the work: "her "broad sympathies, her quick wits, her intuitions and her delight in self sacrifice"" (54). The feminine qualities lauded by the profession are the doubled-edged sword that offered women unprecedented professional opportunity and simultaneously justified their exploitation.

The most telling example connecting the goals of the public library movement to women's work and social reproduction is Dewey's speech to the Association of Collegiate Alumnae in 1886. This was just 10 years after the creation of the ALA and early on in both the public library movement and the feminization of librarianship. This speech, titled "Librarianship as a Profession for College-Bred Women" successfully recruited women to join the first library school, the School of Library Economy, at Columbia University, which opened in 1887. There were a disproportionate number of women in the first library school class: 17 out of the first 20 students. This number anticipates the profession's upcoming demographic shift. Dewey's speech, reprinted in the first issue of *Library Notes*, begins by addressing the social ills that make the public library necessary, and then describes the feminine qualities necessary for redressing these ills. Through his description of the profession and its goals, Dewey positions women's work as the solution to widespread social issues in a way that anticipated some of women's greatest contributions to the profession.

Dewey's speech is ideologically consistent with Carnegie's from the outset and leaves no space to consider alternative solutions to the period's social problems. Like Carnegie, he begins by prescribing education as the solution to widespread social inequality. Dewey frames the expansive public library movement as the popularly accepted solution to the faults in the public education system. He explains that public education is not able to keep up with increasing illiteracy rates for a few reasons, including that "most children must become bread winners before they are taught to take the author's meaning readily from the printed page" (1886, 43). Libraries are able to address these causes of illiteracy by providing communities with access to education at all stages of their lives. To demonstrate that libraries are popularly supported in this goal, Dewey points to the incredible growth of the public library movement and the extensive support it has received from wealthy philanthropists, including Carnegie, Walter Newberry and Enoch Pratt (45). Missing from Dewey's speech is an acknowledgement of the underlying economic conditions that necessitate sending children to work to support their families and abandon their schooling. Dewey's particular style of framing this significant social issue, by identifying rising illiteracy rates as a central problem and literacy as the solution, suggests that the resolution to social upheaval and inequality is attainable and near at hand.

Dewey's argument that libraries can solve these social ills are constructed specifically to appeal to his female audience. Dewey presents the problems with public education and their solutions in library work in terms of which profession—the established female profession of teaching or the emerging profession of librarianship—is better positioned to positively influence the morals and culture of their community. In contrast to teaching, the librarian does not experience the disappointment of having to hear a "bright, promising boy or girl" say "Teacher, I am not coming to school any more. I am going to work in the factory," or "I am going to help mother at home" (52). The librarian has "a school in which the classes graduate only with death" (53). As such, she is able to influence bright boys and girls all their lives. She is also able to "reach and interest people who have never been in the habit of reading; to lead readers into new and more profitable fields, and to create a thirst for better books" (52). Dewey tells his audience of women that if they want to exert moral influence over the lives of the poor, particularly poor children, the library is the best place to do it. By selling library work in this way, Dewey positions the nurturing and morally superior woman as the solution to the scourge of illiteracy.

Librarianship, as represented by Dewey to "college-bred women," offers women the opportunity to fulfill their established social roles and to identify with their work as intimately as a mother identifies with the work of motherhood. Throughout the speech, Dewey draws many explicit parallels between librarianship and missionary work, but the profession he describes has many implicit similarities to motherhood. Librarianship is not merely wage labour he implies, "the librarian puts his heart and life into his work" and "does the work because it is his duty or privilege ... It is his 'vocation'" (Dewey 1886, 51). Like a mother's work, the librarian's work is motivated by the heart, as it appears to be a calling tied to the librarian's innermost identity and the importance of the work itself is put ahead of the librarian's personal needs. Women's work, and mothering in particular, was never complete because it was the same as simply being a woman, which you could not turn off when your shift was over. Librarianship, in Dewey's construction, offered educated women an alternative to motherhood that would still allow them to express their femininity by committing their identities and lifestyles to their work.

Reproducing Gender Inequality

Crucially, Dewey's rhetorical appeal to women through his allusions to motherhood allows him to simultaneously justify and rationalize the incredibly low pay women could expect if they chose librarianship. Dewey says quite a bit on the subject of pay. Immediately following his description of librarianship as a "vocation," Dewey explains that "the selfish considerations of reputation, or personal comfort, or emolument are all secondary" (1886, 51). Presented in this context, the relative poverty of the librarian ties librarianship even tighter to the conception of women's work as natural. In a following section he explains that entry level positions are competitively sought, which keeps salaries down (51). But his female audience has already been given a reason to dismiss this concern. Through her poverty the female librarian could demonstrate her womanly delight in self-sacrifice and commitment to the elevation of the community at her own expense.

Indeed, femininity, as it was defined under industrial capitalism, benefitted capital by producing a separate sphere to produce and maintain the labour force, but it also profitably complicated the relation of female wage earners to the labour market. Gonzalez points out that despite women's ideological banishment to the domestic sphere, they have taken part in the waged workforce as long as it has existed, and their exploitation as wage labourers has consistently taken a different form than men's. She proposes a materially grounded explanation: "The sexual segregation of work in the capitalist mode of production is directly related to the temporality of a woman's life: as the bearer of children" (2011, 228). She continues to explain that women's participation in the labor market clearly follows the typical reproductive cycle of a woman's life. As a result, women are consistently relegated to temporary and part-time work. This precarity in the job market then reinforces "a society-wide commitment to and ideology about women's natural place, both in the home and at work" (229). Dewey confirms Gonzalez's assessment when, in an article in *Library Notes*, he explains that "with women the probability or even the possibility that her position is only temporary and that she will soon leave for home life does more than anything else to keep her value down" (1979, 11). Here, Lerner's claim, that while women have not had the power to write their own histories they have always been actors and agents in history, resurfaces, and with Gonzalez' argument

41

in mind it seems absolutely, and even a little cruelly, apt: women have always been actors and agents in history because through physical and social reproduction they have been the force behind each mode of production's ability to reproduce itself. The modification of Schiller's argument follows directly from this insight. Women were recruited into librarianship as both a source of cheap labour, due to their history *outside the workforce*, and because they seemed to fit the emerging role of librarian so well, due to their secret history *of reproducing the workforce*.

Concluding Notes

Joanne Passet argues that women of this period did not passively accept the low pay of librarianship, but despite their efforts, librarians' salaries were low and women librarians' salaries were even lower. The first public library union emerged in 1917 with sex discrimination at the top of their list of grievances.[12] Anti-unionists called them "materialistic," "self-serving" and "unfeminine" (Garrison 1979, 229). In 1920, the University of Washington library school director editorialized that union tactics for improving salaries were inappropriate for librarians and would result in "loss of the spirit, and the dignity" (quoted in Passet 1996, 213). In that same year, wallpaper hangers and milk truck drivers went on strike to raise their salaries to $10 a day, while "women librarians could expect to earn $40 to $75 a month" (Passet 1996, 209). In Garrison's words, women librarians could expect to settle "along with their unskilled, uneducated, and poor counterparts—to the bottom of the American working world" (1979, 183). Adhering to the anti-union sentiment ingrained in the middle-class femininity of the period, the majority of women librarians could expect lives of harsh poverty, instability and little chance of social mobility.

Early women librarians were not only subject to the unfortunate material conditions of the working class, but as women professionals they were subject to individualist rhetoric that undermined their perceptions of structural inequality. A 1912 speech to a class of graduating college women by ALA president Herbert Putnam,

---

12 *See* Christine Shanley's "The Library Employees' Union of Greater New York, 1917-1929." For the unique story of the brief emergence of a library union run by radical feminists that identified the labour issues of librarians as feminist issues.

full of advice on how women could best advance their careers, has distinct parallels to Carnegie's speech to the working men in 1889. Just as Carnegie encouraged his workers to understand the economic laws that shaped their experiences at work, Putnam encourages his audience to think outside themselves and keep in view "the larger whole" (1979, 62). Preempting their future complaints that they have not been given a fair chance to move ahead, Putnam explains that women are responsible for their own stagnant careers, and if they want to improve they should aspire to "manliness" and take more initiative. A man, for Putnam, recognizes that "behind any act which affects him or his authority ... there may be, there probably are, considerations larger than himself, larger, perhaps, than his superior who makes the decision, and imperative upon the later" (57). Luckily, from Putnam's point of view, unsatisfied women professionals have recourse to the public library, for "there is no study rightly pursed which is not vocational" (63). Again, individual self-improvement is posited as the reasonable alternative to addressing and altering structural inequalities, and public libraries become the solution to the problem of professional women's social mobility.

The education about "the larger whole" that the early public library offered its patrons necessarily excluded any perspectives that might suggest or promote the possibility of dividing labour between the classes or the genders in a different, or equally beneficial, way. The ideologues of capital encouraged both workers and women to accept their social and economic position and struggle on an individual level to become the exception to the rule of "inequality of environment." Alternative interpretations of social strife and alternative models of library service that emphasized collective support and collective improvement existed in the period (such as the KoL), but they were unknown or passed over as the library movement and its increasingly female staff drew its legitimation from the existing structures of power. The influence and opportunity women librarians gained from their role as social reproducers in this period was justification enough for them to support capital's interests and work simultaneously to reproduce their own subordination. Rather than try to undermine the agency of early women librarians, this paper hopes to offer a version of the history of the feminization of librarianship that identifies the ideological limits that worked against the idealistic goals of the progressive women of the profession. This paper is optimistic, in the spirit of Lerner, that knowledge of history can be a meaningful force in the shaping of the future.

Recognizing that capitalist ideology has deeply influenced public librarianship from its beginning casts in a new light the truism that technological advances and the creation of an "information economy" have repositioned the public libraries of today such that they must now more actively demonstrate their social and economic value to their funders. New technologies and the information economy instead have thrown into relief the *continuing* connection between private interests and public librarianship. Now, as in the past, public libraries' value is derived at least in part from their ability to prepare a workforce for existing economic conditions. Further research towards understanding the socially reproductive influence of public libraries could beneficially explore the relationship between early public libraries and racialized inequality in the labour market or contemporary public libraries as they encounter the global workforce.

The labour market today is characterized by the need for flexible workers: full time positions are harder to find while part time and contract work with no job security proliferate. Guy Standing describes the emergence of the "precariat" a "*class-in-the-making*" defined by its flexibility and lack of access to the types of labour-related security that unions and labour parties fought for throughout the 20th century (2011, 7, author's italics). Though library unions have worked hard to reduce inequality in the profession, the difficulty of making a living in the global labour market is experienced by librarians and library users alike. Madeline Schwartz notes the similarity between contemporary flexible workers and their un-unionized, insecure and low-paying jobs and women's historic relation to wage labour (2013, para. 11). Public libraries' goal of improving quality of life for their users through access to information and services remains noble and worthwhile, but it is a timely moment to reflect on the historical roots of the goal of social mobility and the structural possibility of achieving it in a meaningful way.

WORKS CITED

Arnove, Robert F. 1980. "Introduction." In *Philanthropy and Cultural Imperialism: The Foundations at Home and Abroad*. Boston, Mass: G. K. Hall.

Bowles, Samuel and Herbert Gintis. 2011. *Schooling in Capitalist America: Educational Reform and the Contradictions of Economic Life*. Chicago, IL: Haymarket Books.

Carnegie, Andrew. 1968. "The Common Interest of Labor and Capital: Address to Workingmen." In *The Empire of Business*, 57-73. New York, NY: Greenwood.

—. "The Gospel of Wealth." 1889. Carnegie Corporation of New York. Accessed January 18, 2013. https://www.carnegie.org/about/our-history/gospelofwealth/.

Cutler Fairchild, Salome. 1979. "Women in American Libraries." In *The Role of Women in Librarianship, 1876 – 1976: the Entry, Advancement, and Struggle for Equalization in one Profession*, edited by Kathleen Weibel and Kathleen M. Heim, 48-55. Phoenix: Oryx Press.

Dalla Costa, Mariarosa and Selma James. 1972. *The Power of Women and the Subversion of the Community*. London, UK: Falling Wall Press.

Dana, John Cotton. 1896. "Library Primer." *Public Libraries* 1 (1): 5-10.

Dewey, Melvil. 1886. "Notes from 'Librarianship as a Profession for College-Bred Women.'" *Library Notes* 1 (1): 43-53.

—. 1979. "Women in Libraries: How they are Handicapped." In *The Role of Women in Librarianship, 1876 – 1976: the Entry, Advancement, and Struggle for Equalization in One Profession*, edited by Kathleen Weibel and Kathleen M. Heim, 10-12. Phoenix: Oryx Press.

Eastman, Linda A. 1897. "Aims and Personal Attitude in Library Work." *Library Journal* 22: 80.Federici, Sylvia. 2004. *Caliban and the Witch: Women, the Body and Primitive Accumulation.* Brooklyn. MY: Autonomedia.

Garrison, Dee. 1979. *Apostles of Culture.* New York, NY: The Free Press.

Gonzalez, Maya Andrea. 2011. "Communization and the Abolition of Gender." In *Communization and its Discontents,* edited by Benjamin Noys, 219-34. New York: Minor Compositions.

Harris, Michael. 1982. "The Purpose of the American Public Library: A Revisionist Interpretation of History." In *Public Librarianship: A Reader,* edited by Jane Robbins-Carter, 63-73. Littleton, Colorado: Libraries Unlimited.

Harris, Roma M. 1992. *Librarianship: The Erosion of a Woman's Profession.* Norwood, NJ: Ablex Publishing Co.

Hildenbrand, Suzanne. 1985. "Ambiguous Authority and Aborted Ambition: Gender, Professionalism and the Rise and Fall of the Welfare State." *Library Trends* Fall: 185-198. https://www.ideals.illinois.edu/bitstream/handle/2142/7422/librarytrendsv34i2d_opt.pdf?sequence=1.

James, Selma. 1972. "Introduction." In *The Power of Women and the Subversion of the Community.* London, UK: Falling Wall Press.

Lerner, Gerda. 1986. *The Creation of Patriarchy.* New York, NY: Oxford University Press.

Maack, Mary Niles. 1998. "Gender, Culture and the Transformation of American Librarianship, 1890-1920." *Libraries & Culture* 33 (Winter): 51-61. http://www.jstor.org/stable/25548597.

Malone, Cheryl Knott. 1996. "Women's Unpaid Work in Libraries: Change and Continuity." In *Reclaiming the American Library Past: Writing Women In,* edited by Suzanne Hildenbrand, 279-99. Norwood, NJ: Ablex.

Martin, Robert S. 1993. *Carnegie Denied: Communities Rejecting Carnegie Library Construction grants, 1898-1925.* Westport, Conn.: Greenwood Press.

Marx, Karl. 1990. *Capital Volume 1: A Critique of Political Economy.* London, UK: Penguin Classics.

Olsen, Hope A. and Amber Ritchie. 2006. "Introduction: Gentility, Technicality, and Salary: Women in the Literature of Librarianship." In *On Account of Sex: An Annotated Bibliography on the Status of Women in Librarianship 1998 -2002,* edited by Betsy Kruger and Catherine Larson. Lanham, MD: Scarecrow Press.

Passet, Joanne E. 1996. "You Don't Have to Pay Librarians." In *Reclaiming the American Library Past: Writing Women In,* edited by Suzanne Hildenbrand, 207-19. Norwood, NJ: Ablex.

Pawley, Christine. 1998. "Hegemony's Handmaid? The Library and Information Studies Curriculum from a Class Perspective." *Library Quarterly* 68 (2): 123-144. http://www.jstor.org/stable/4309200.

Putnam, Herbert. 1979. "The Prospect: An Address Before a Graduating Class of Women." 1912. In *The Role of Women in Librarianship, 1876 – 1976: the Entry, Advancement, and Struggle for Equalization in One Profession,* edited by Kathleen Weibel and Kathleen M. Heim, 56-66. Phoenix: Oryx Press.

Scobey, David. 1984. "Boycotting the Politics Factory: Labor Radicalism and The New York City Mayoral Election of 1884." *Radical History Review* 28-30: 280-325. doi: 10.1215/01636545-1984-28-30-280.

Schiller, Anita. 1974. "Women in Librarianship." In *Advances in Librarianship, vol. 4,* edited by Melvin J. Voight, 103-47. New York, NY: Academic Press.

Schwartz, Madeleine. 2013. "Opportunity Costs: The True Price of Internships." *Dissent: A Quarterly of Politics and Culture* Winter. https://www.dissentmagazine.org/article/opportunity-costs-the-true-price-of-internships.

Shanley, Catherine. 1995. "The Library Employees' Union of Greater New York, 1917-1929." *Libraries & Culture* 30 (3): 235-264. http://www.jstor.org/stable/25542770.

Sigerman, Harriet. 2000. "Laborers for Liberty 1865-1890." In *No Small Courage: A History of Women in the United States*, edited by Nancy F. Cott, 289-352. New York, NY: Oxford University Press.

Standing, Guy. 2011. *The Precariat: The New Dangerous Class*. Huntingdon, GBR: Bloomsbury.Stauffer, Suzanne. 2006. "Introduction." In *Library Daylight: Tracings of Modern Librarianship, 1874-1922*, edited by Rory Litwin, 1-11. Duluth, MN: Library Juice Press.

Stevenson, Siobhan A. 2005. "The Post-Fordist Public Library: from Carnegie to Gates." PhD diss., University of Western Ontario.

Swinton, John. 1894. *Striking for Life: Labor's Side of the Labor Question, the Right of the Workingman to a Fair Living and Articles Specially Contributed by Samuel Gompers, Eugene V. Debs, John W. Hayes*. New York?: American Manufacturing and Publishing Co. Internet Archive.

Valentine, Jolie. 2005. "Our Community, Our Library: Women, Schools, and Popular Culture in the Public Library Movement." *Public Library Quarterly* 24(4): 45-79.

Van Slyck, Abigail A. 1995. *Free to All: Carnegie Libraries & American Culture 1890-1920*. Chicago and London: University of Chicago Press.

Weibel, Kathleen and Kathleen M. Heim, eds. 1979. "Introduction." In *The Role of Women in Librarianship, 1876 – 1976: the Entry, Advancement, and Struggle for Equalization in One Profession*, xiv-xxv. Phoenix: Oryx Press.

From Steam Engines to Search Engines: Class Struggle in an Information Economy

Amanda Bird and Braden Cannon

Introduction

The North American economy of the late 19th and early 20th century was largely dependent upon resource extraction (e.g. mining) and transportation networks (e.g. rail and shipping) that linked financial hubs over wide distances across the continent. Because of this dependence, workers in those sectors were sometimes able to shut down the entire economy or large sectors therein through concerted and deliberate actions such as strikes, boycotts, and occupations. Such actions were led by unions and organizers in rail, mines, shipping, general transport, and related industries and resulted in a series of struggles that have been termed "labor wars" (Lens 2009) and that have come to define labor history from the 1870s to the 1930s.[1]

Schmidt and van der Walt note that the era of labor struggle

took place in an earlier phase of globalisation, marked by high levels of international economic integration and free

---

1   The era of labor wars started with the Great Railroad Strike of 1877 and continued through the 1886 general strike for the 8-hour day, the Pullman Strike of 1894, the Western Federation of Miners conflagrations of the 1900s, the Colorado Coal Wars of the 1910s, the Seattle and Winnipeg General Strikes of 1919, the Minneapolis Teamsters strike of 1934, and the San Francisco General Strike of 1934 among many other incidents. For more information about this era of labor history and these events specifically, see Adamic; Brecher; and Lens.

trade, immigration, rapid advances in telecommunications and transport, and the rise of supranational institutions, including early transnational corporations. This is a period distant in time, but in many ways not so different from the twenty-first century world of neoliberalism. (2009, 14)

As will be discussed below, the current economy can be understood to be an information economy that defines an entire information society. If this is true, then information workers could be as strategically poised for collective action that can profoundly affect or even redirect the economy through organized, class struggle. Is the information society, built on an information economy, so fundamentally different from a 19th century economy built on resource extraction and transportation? And if so, are information workers uniquely poised to strike at the heart of this new economy the way that rail workers and miners were able to shut down the economy through collective action in the late 1800s and early 1900s?

Despite similarities between these eras and the seemingly perfect placement of information workers in an information economy, library and information workers do not in fact have the same economic power that resource and transportation workers once had. Through an exploration of the information economy; the commodification of information; deprofessionalization of the information sector; and information sector unions and professional associations, we examine why information workers do not have the same ability to incite sudden and catalytic economic upheaval the way that resource and transportation workers did in past centuries.

Information Economy

Having a clear concept of what comprises an information economy is difficult, but a clear understanding is important. Porat explains that an information economy exists when "labor related to information (e.g., creation, processing, dissemination) begins to exceed work related to the other three economic sectors (i.e., agriculture, industry, and service)" (qtd. in Pemberton 1995). Information *work* then, can be defined as when a "worker's main task involve[s] information processing or manipulation in any form, such as information production, recycling, or maintenance" (Pemberton 1995). Pemberton goes on to explain what is produced by information work:

> [T]he consequence of information work is more information, whether in the form of new knowledge or repackaged existing forms. Unlike the assembly line worker, an information worker, such as a telephone operator, processes and manipulates information as an end in itself. Information defines the task, the product, and the worker.

Although computers played a major role in the information economy after 1950, Pemberton argues that it is the need for *workers* and their work, not the tools, that had the most direct bearing on the initial emergence of the information economy. An economy based on information, that is, an economy based on who creates, controls, retrieves, understands, and shares information, and on how information can be commodified through the division of labor, potentially places information workers in a revolutionary position.

In the 1920s, information workers began overtaking agricultural workers in conjunction with the rise of modern management and the rising knowledge class, leading to a direct relationship between information, knowledge acquisition, classism, and capitalist ideologies (Pemberton 1995). Pemberton explains that as the industrial period (and its economic sector) reached its height, so too did a parallel rise in the need for the management of information. Beginning in the late 1950s and early 1960s, the transition from a predominantly manufacturing economy to that of an information economy arose (Godin 2008). This major socio-cultural and socio-economic shift evolved in tandem with the way the concept of information was understood in relation to capital. This understanding is characterized by three evolving stages: information as knowledge, information as commodity, and information as technology (Godin 2008). Information as knowledge, as it was characterized in the 1950s, centered on the rapid growth of scientific and technological information. Godin writes that there was an "explosion of literature" (2008, 256), and that computers were seen as the best solution to store and retrieve this literature. At the time, there were concerns with using computers, due to the "too-rapid development" of computer information systems and the related risk that complications could arise due to "system incompatibility," resulting in the need for information management and for "appropriate technological systems to process it" (256).

Information as an economic commodity manifested in the late 1970s and early 1980s, when policy-makers became heavily focused on structural changes in the economy. Their primary focus was on "the transition from a manufacturing economy to a service or information economy" (Godin 2008, 256). As the economy of industry reached its height, a simultaneous rise in the need for information management arose in order to control costs, measure the efficacy of labor-saving initiatives, and coordinate de-centralized enterprises (Pemberton 1995).

The third stage in thinking about information was a direct result of the management of information: information as technology. Godin writes: "Many analysts came to view information technologies, because of their widespread effects on the economy, as bringing forth a new techo-economic paradigm or technological revolution" (2008, 256). The notion that information is technology, and that it is the driving force in the production of diverse forms of labor, is profound. Godin writes, "the computer can be considered as the key to the second industrial revolution, just as the steam engine was the center of the first industrial revolution" (255). The steam engine was literally the driving force in the emerging capitalist economy; the information economy has now replaced this driver of capitalist enterprise.

COMMODIFICATION OF INFORMATION

Information is a commodity and the people involved in its creation, organization, retrieval, transmission and preservation (for the purposes of this paper, librarians, archivists and other information workers) are commodities themselves. Our labor – what we do as information workers – is a product that contributes to capitalist economies. The product that we create, however, is unique and cannot be seen through the same lens as those goods that are manufactured and produced on assembly lines. Commercial goods are purpose-built whereas the utility of information can shift based on the actions or motivations of the end user or the context in which the information is made available (e.g. the level and quality of descriptive data applied to the information, the mandate of the institution housing the information, etc.).

Leadbeater frames the knowledge economy as "new capital," by arguing that the shift of economic assets moves from "traditional physical assets" towards those that are intangible: human capital, research, and development (1998, 377). The notion of "new capital," however, isn't new at all. There has always been an inseparable connection between labor, knowledge, and the goods that both produce: the shift is in the value ascribed to labor and knowledge. The physical goods that are produced by labor – cars, iPhones, furniture, is finite. One car is always one car. Dividing the labor to create one car into its component parts is one way that the owners of the product can create that product as cheaply as possible, and more importantly, retain the power related to knowing how to recreate it. Dividing labor isn't just an effective way to produce goods quickly; it is also an effective way to limit a worker's understanding of that which they produce. Information, however, is not finite, and the question of who owns the product that information generates is not always clear: what the information economy produces is not one car, one iPhone, or one piece of furniture. The information economy creates the concept of intellectual property and the commodification of process (i.e. how a business operates has become as equally important as what that business produces or provides – consider the success of the marketing of Apple Inc. as a maverick organization that does things differently from other businesses).

The economic value of information, then, is arbitrarily determined based on the socially constructed value of the product or service created from that information. In their article, Fine, Jeong, and Gong discuss the complexity of the knowledge economy and its relationship to capitalism and class structure. They write: "The knowledge economy is extremely diverse in terms of functions and substance, ranging across the enhancing of productivity, the generation of new products and processes, and the governance of economic, social and ideological reproduction" (2010, 71). What the information economy unifies, however, is the treatment of all information as a source of profit that must be owned and protected. Even corporate identity becomes a hotly contested commodity.

The work of librarians, archivists, and other information workers has a somewhat contradictory role in this information economy. Their work is based to a large degree on the description of information and making it available for wide use. Information workers, then, can be understood as interlocutors. They are the intermediaries who connect people to information, which can then be commodified or put to some other use. This information we locate, however, isn't produced by us – it is made available by us. Information workers are synthesizers – they connect individual elements of data, of information, and assist people in enhancing their understanding. This work, with its emphasis on openness and availability, stands outside the guarded economy of intellectual property in a manner altogether alien to the work of resource or transportation workers and its intrinsic relation to the industrial age economy. Simply put, information workers are anomalies in an information economy: their work runs counter to the dominant ideologies of property, control, and profit. As such, information workers in an information economy cannot approach the level of economic power that resource and transportation workers had over their industrial economy.

ORGANIZATIONAL CULTURE

Although the potential role of information workers in wider class struggle within an information economy is very limited, the traditional division of labor and the exploitation of that labor in capitalist organizations exist in libraries and archives, as well. In order to accurately look at the labor of information workers in connection to capitalist economy, a close examination of the hierarchies and organizational culture within libraries is warranted.

One divide in libraries is between professional librarians and library assistants.[2] The term "professional" itself requires contemplation and clarification. Adams states that professions are typically understood as "occupations with special status as experts and/or moral authorities [...], often as a result of extensive educations, training and licensing" (2012, 328). Adams goes on to interpret professionalism through a Foucauldian lens when she writes that professionalism is seen as a "field of knowledge constituted through a set of discursive practices and formations, and which cuts across institutions to share and reify a particular way of knowing the world" (328). Bayles mentions three

---

2   Library assistants may also be referred to as paraprofessionals, library technicians, or other terms within different institutions. For the purposes of this paper, a professional librarian is an individual who holds a Master's Degree in Library and Information Studies or equivalent degree.

traits that define a professional: "extensive training, a significant intellectual component, and a trained ability that puts one in a position to provide an important service to society" (qtd. in Froleich 1998). Librarians are not required to have a license in order to work as librarians; one could argue that a similar set of discursive practices exists between professional librarians and library assistants in order to have a shared epistemology, and on-the-job training for librarians is just as essential for the practice of competent librarianship as it is to be a competent library assistant.

The division between librarians and library assistants contributes to the inability of information workers to drive change within their work force the way that resource workers have succeeded in doing. For those information workers who fall within the scope of being identified as professional librarians and archivists, an element of prestige surrounds our work. We are, generally speaking, given more autonomy in our work, the scope of our work in terms of contributions that impact the organization we work for is greater than that of library assistants, we have more professional development opportunities, and we are also more easily able to qualify for and be appointed to positions of greater authority and income. There is, however, a downside to these opportunities when we look at our role within an organizational culture that adheres and contributes to rigid hierarchies. Adams notes, "professionalism, for all the ways in which it is invoked with positivity, also hides processes of marginalization" (2012, 328). Information workers who do not fall under the category of professional librarian are paid less than librarians, and are typically supervised by librarians, some of whom hold management positions within their organizations. This divide, based on socially constructed merits on differing types of education (an MLIS versus a technician diploma) can result in a schism between professional and non-professional library workers. Rather than a feeling of unity and camaraderie among all information workers, there is a divide between who is a librarian and who is not; a divided workforce faces significant challenges when it comes to building solidarity amongst workers in the face of austerity measures, workers' rights, and advocating for the essential services that information workers provide.

The other significant hierarchy within libraries is that of librarians and administrators. From the perspective of library assistants, librarians may be seen as administrators because the scope of librarians' work is typically broader than that of library assistants, whose primary responsibility is to run the day-to-day operations of libraries. Librarians typically have a higher profile within their organizations because the work they do has a broader scope and there is a greater responsibility to conform to and fulfill the strategic goals of their respective institutions. On this topic, Marshall states: "people who are employed within such institutions [libraries] are expected to conform to the mission statements and institutional rules which establish procedures, culture and 'ethics' for all employees" (2008, 154). Library assistants see librarians as authority figures and not necessarily as allies; librarians may themselves feel a sense of obligation and responsibility to clearly align with the institutional culture of their organizations. Because librarians typically work very closely with upper management and administrators, there is often a comfortable and sincere feeling of collegiality between them. This level of professionalism, however, and the professional identity that accompanies it, contributes to marginalization. Librarians are stuck in the middle of the hierarchy and struggle to be recognized as workers by their library assistant colleagues; library administrators benefit from the skill and expertise of librarians to carry out strategic goals and other mandates – librarians are seen as workers by administrators, but are not seen this way by other workers. Solidarity and a unified voice among workers are virtually impossible to develop within workplace hierarchies that place differing levels of value on the work of library workers, be they paraprofessionals or professional librarians. The relationships librarians have with other information workers and with administrators are, in a word, nebulous.

DEPROFESSIONALIZATION

This lack of workplace identity is contributing to the devaluation of libraries. Without a unified voice, advocating for libraries and for library workers is virtually impossible. Add to this the disturbing reality that many library administrators in key decision-making positions are not in fact librarians themselves, and the value of the intellectual labor of library workers, and the significance of libraries themselves, is further diminished. In his article, Froehlich asks, "Is it fair that nonlibrarians are hired as directors of libraries when in many cases their lack of experience of library functions and operations makes them ill-suited as administrators, personnel directors, or public relations officers?" (1998) The question is obviously rhetorical, but raises a question of its own: why are non-librarians hired to lead libraries? An accountant or economist certainly wouldn't be hired to be the chief of surgery at a hospital, and a dentist wouldn't be hired to be a Supreme Court judge. The answer is due to a lack of understanding the role of information workers which results in an inaccurate but widespread public perception that libraries are unimportant and the work of librarians and other information workers is no longer necessary: why have librarians work as information synthesizers when Google can do that work from the comfort of home?

To combat this perception, some library boards hire non-librarian professionals into executive positions to provide a higher level of visibility or cachet to a library system; unfortunately, this move does the opposite of its intention. Froehlich writes, "from the viewpoint of the governing board, such hires bring prestige to the organization and may encourage increased funding, patronage, and visibility" (1998). This decision is often based on the social utility principle, whereby the objective of creating social harmony within an organization is paramount. Governing bodies may argue that "such hires will promote the overall goals of the organization in the long run" (Froehlich 1998). The result of these hires, however, is typically negative:

> Nonlibrarian directors or supervisors, while they could be made sensitive to library issues, tend to have the lowest level of knowledge of a library's operations and often base their decision on a grossly inaccurate image of the library[...]. It also devalues the profession because it may imply that professionals are not good enough to run prestigious libraries. (Drake, qtd. in Froehlich, 1998)

Froehlich goes on to explain that although professional librarians may have concerns about these decisions, including a sense of ethical unease regarding hiring practices, they seldom voice their concerns, so as to avoid disharmony. Why the concern over creating disharmony? The reason: collegiality among administrators and an ambivalent and ambiguous professional identity. Non-professional library workers don't necessarily see professional librarians as colleagues; professional librarians have a higher level of visibility in their organizations than other library workers and may have a heightened sense of responsibility toward library administrators than other information workers. This gets at the heart of class struggle in the information field context. Although there are varying degrees of education, skill, and training found among the entirety of information workers, they are still linked through the commonality of having to sell their labor and work within an organization over which they have no control. Furthermore, all library staff are subject to the devolution of the role of librarians and other information workers through the deskilling and devaluing of their intellectual labor. The inability or unwillingness of all information workers to recognize these commonalities helps maintain a divisive workplace and prevents unity among workers and the potential of using collective action to settle labor disputes effectively.

Digital Labor

Information work is increasingly digital, but does this digital shift fundamentally alter the nature of the work or relations between workers and administrators? Blom, Melin, and Pyöriä argue that the mere use of digital technology is not enough to define work as information work and that "[j]ob autonomy is one of the most important positive expectations attached to information work" (2002, 335, 339). While there is a certain level of autonomy attached to information work in library and archives settings, information workers of all kinds are still beholden to administrative decisions made without consultation and the distribution of resources based on these decisions. In light of this power imbalance, autonomy is both limited in scope and ultimately illusory. In fact, Lee goes so far as to argue that "the lived realities of the vast majority of white-collar work tend to bear out Marx's original proletarianization thesis in which white-collar labor is increasingly subjected to the same forms of routinization, discipline, and authoritarian control as its more traditional blue-collar counterpart" (2005, 24). Professional librarians are as beholden to administrative structures as their library assistant colleagues and actions that can appear to be relatively autonomous (e.g. the management of library social media accounts or purchases of collections) are actually defined and restricted by institutional communications policies, budgetary decisions, or human resources policies that are kept out of the control of information workers.

Furthermore, the development of information work in relation to the expansion of digital technology "[has] not occurred in a vacuum; [it is] unfolding against existing contradictions between public and private interests, between labor and capital" (Jones 2010, 537). Mills (2010, 534), Jones (537), and Schenk and Anderson (qtd. in Worman and Samek 2011, 73) have observed that digital technology is another tool that can be used by management to out-source labor, replace full-time staff with tenuous contract work, and for the private accumulation of profit, respectively. These are not new issues in capitalist relations but rather the repetition and reinforcement of existing relationships based on exploitation, but with new technologies at the disposal of management.

Digital technologies and the labor associated with them do provide one new facet: the creative ability to obscure the social relationships of capitalism (King 2010, 299). As noted above, information work, particularly that work organized around laboring digitally, is often associated with job autonomy but that autonomy is predicated on the same capitalist relationships and their concomitant power imbalances. A programmer working for an innovative, new start-up in Silicon Valley, for instance, may benefit from a certain expectancy of flexibility and independence, but that flexibility only eases the constraints implicit in selling ones labor for wages. The constraints are sufficiently relaxed to prevent workers from questioning the capitalist relationships within the organization, but those relationships are still present and unaltered. There is simply a digital veneer of independence over the same hierarchies that have been imposed on wage laborers since the rise of capitalism.

Information work (at least that performed by librarians, archivists, and related workers) does not exist at the point of production but instead manages and organizes the product of others' labor. That is not to say that the output of information workers' labor cannot be commodified and therefore exploited for profit; on the contrary, Barbrook contends that corporate leaders believe that the "future of capitalism lies in the commodification of information," which can be monetized only through the labor of information workers (2005). That does not alter the fact that the information work done in library, archives, and similar settings does not directly contribute to generating profit and is "consigned to the margins of the 'information' society in the twenty first century" (Muddiman, qtd. in Durrani and Smallwood 2006, 6). This marginalization occurs to an extent that resource and transportation workers of the late 1800s and early 1900s never experienced because their labor was directly connected to the profits of industry and were thus able to directly interfere with the efficient management and profit-generating capacities of their economy.

PROFESSIONALISM AS DIVISIVE IDEOLOGY

The above-noted marginalization of information workers is not the only impediment to effective assaults on capitalism. Whereas the resource and transportation workers discussed previously started with the base assumption that they were *workers* and members of a wider, working class movement, such a starting point is seemingly absent from the library and information sector. Simply put, librarians and related workers who possess a graduate degree do not usually identify as workers but rather as "professionals." This identification is not always self-applied, however, but encouraged by library schools and professional associations. Indeed, the existence of professional associations is an impediment to the creation of a working class identity within the library and information workforce as it creates splits in the interests of library and information workers. Raju, Stilwell, and Leach note that library and information workers have their interests divided between unions that address industrial issues and professional associations that address library and information concerns (2006, 208). No such divide exists within work forces unified into one labor movement devoid of professional pretensions. Furthermore, support staff within the library and information sector "could see, as preferable, an organization that would represent their specific support staff interests as opposed to an organization that would represent the interests of the profession. For instance, the primary interests of the support staff centre around the industrial issues affecting the sector" (209). A union and only a union, therefore, is the primary means of organization for support staff as it would be for any worker whose only capital is his or her labor that must be sold for a wage, professionals included.

However, not all workers deemed professionals are blind to the problems with professional associations. In a study conducted in 1992, Anderson, D'Amicantonio, and Dubois found that the majority of surveyed librarians would rather leave their professional association than their union (1992). A survey conducted by Raju, Stilwell, and Leach in 2006 reported that most respondents found their professional associations too meek when aggression and assertion are required to protect the interests of its members (212). And then there is this blunt assessment offered decades ago but is still relevant today: "Professionalism is an ideology which prevents librarians from organizing into unions, obscures the fundamental difference between labor and management within library organizations, and creates tension and conflict between librarians and their clients" (Estabrook 1981, 125). Since those words were written, the ideology of professionalism has consumed information work to the extent that students of graduate programs in library and information studies are trained to be managers as much as they are to be librarians or archivists, further obscuring the stark differences between what librarians actually control and that which is controlled by administrators. The more that information workers holding graduate degrees identify with their administration, the less cohesive the labor force becomes.

Awareness of the divisiveness caused by professional associations is not enough to counter it or to build class-consciousness within the library and information sector. This is especially true when considering that professionalism as an identity is specifically used as a wedge to divide workers, both by management and workers themselves. For instance, the first attempt to organize a union within the Chicago Public Library in 1922 was thwarted by a management-organized professional association that prevented the formation of a true union in that institution for another 15 years (Latham 2008, 18). The closing of salary gaps between different segments of workers, perceived or actual, is another wedge used to propagate an elitist elevation of professionals above support staff and prevents solidarity within a strong union (Estabrook 1981, 126). Professional associations act to define and segregate one segment of the library and information workforce as having a special skill-set that is so rarefied as to exist in a vacuum, whereas support staff are interchangeable. Some even argue that support staff do not even share the same values as professionalized librarians and use scare tactics such as automation to further divide those workers with graduate degrees from those without:

> Increased automation has decreased the amount of skilled judgment needed to perform many jobs. This had been particularly true in technical services: work once performed only by professional librarians is not routinely

done by paraprofessionals. This makes economic sense for the administration: paraprofessionals are less expensive to employ. However, the values that professional librarians bring to their work, are missing. Inherent in these values is service to the profession as well as the individual institution. We are not only employees of the library, we are part of a profession with a rich history and shared ethics. By contractually defining our status, unions protect our standing as highly educated academic professionals separated by function and responsibilities from nonlibrarians. (Wood 1999, 14)

A labor movement based on solidarity and mutual trust cannot possibly be built on the attitudes expressed above, in which unions are glorified professional associations designed to contractually create a separate, more dignified segment of workers, and in which librarians and similar workers with graduate degrees serve their own profession and its elevated standing instead of the communities in which they work. For example, issues such as automation that affect the entire workforce across all sectors are narrowly defined by Wood as a threat only to the privileged positions held by "professional librarians" and used as a catalyst to further isolate oneself from the "paraprofessionals" who, Wood claims, do not even share the same values. This is indeed rhetoric of class struggle, but only in that it supports the management class because it acts to tear apart solidarity among workers.

The above quote serves to show the most egregious problem with professionalism-as-ideology from a class struggle perspective: though some in the library and information sector (particularly some of those with graduate degrees) may see themselves as special and entitled to be treated as such, the fact is that professionalism has created this illusion and it does not benefit information workers as a united workforce. Instead, it blinds *workers* into identifying with management in a sense of contrived collegiality. Library schools strive to instill a management identity on students, and upon graduation, many entrants into the library and information workforce are inclined to see themselves as partners with not only their direct management, but the entire administrative structure above them. By pointing to graduate degrees and pleading for preferential treatment separate from information workers who do not have the same credentials, the workers' movement is divided and weakened. By gathering with management in those professional associations that are not welcoming to support staff, solidarity is made impossible.

Massive and successful labor movements of the past, including those previously discussed in our introduction, were not hampered by such institutionalized collaboration between privileged segments of the workforce and management as seen in professional associations. The Great Railroad Strike of 1877, for instance, is impossible to imagine occurring under such circumstances in that it took cooperation and solidarity between multiple segments of the rail industry, skilled and unskilled, to bring into being.

INFORMATION WORKERS AND UNIONS

The most successful recourse to effective results for information workers who believe in class struggle is through collective action among all information workers. This collective action can and should take place within pre-existing unions, but the mainstream union movement is not the only option for organizing, as will be discussed below. Considering that they are a well-established presence across the library and information sector, unions, where they exist, are a much more relevant starting point for class-conscious activism than professional associations.

Rates of union membership across the United States workforce have been steadily declining over the past three decades, with the rate of unionization falling from 23.3 percent in the early 1980s to 16.2 in the mid-1990s (Garcha and Phillips 2001, 123). By 2012, that rate had fallen to a new low of 11.3 percent (Bureau of Labor Statistics 2012). However, during this same period the rates of union membership within the library and information sector have steadily risen and are much higher than the wider rates. From 1986 to 1996, the unionization rate among librarians, archivists, and curators rose from 25.6 percent to 32.7 percent (Garcha and Phillips 2001, 123). In 2012, the rate among library occupations is the highest of any sector in the US workforce at 35.4 percent, over three times the national rate (Bureau of Labor Statistics 2012).

While such a high density of union membership in the library and information sector does not guarantee class consciousness, it is certainly a head start. But when looking at the reasons for the growth of the union movement in this sector, patterns focused on class struggle emerge. Guyton argues that a primary cause for unionization among librarians comes from an "awareness of an incongruence between desired and realized job status," postulating that library unions arise from "status ideology" rather than class consciousness (1975, 164). The evidence does not support this view, however. Garcha and Phillips note that protection from arbitrary action by management is a key reason given for librarians joining unions, even above wages (2001, 123); librarians most committed to and active in their unions tend to place a higher value on the principles of the profession (Hovekamp 1997); and the initial growth spurt of unionism in the library and information sector began in a time of economic prosperity, the mid-1960s, and was not purely the result of wage issues but rather a struggle for workers' *control* of library administration (Michener 1976, 171).

The struggle for control is essential to class consciousness: once an information worker realizes that despite collegial relationships shared with management, decisions over the application of resources and therefore the direction of the institution are firmly controlled by management, and that s/he is just another worker selling his/her labor for wages, class identity and solidarity becomes possible. Garcha and Phillips note that "one common goal of librarians [in joining unions] had been the sharing or displacement of administrative authority" (2001, 127), while Guyton shows how the organization of the Los Angeles Public Library Union was "a search by a group of librarians for greater control over their own profession and an exploration of unionism as a vehicle for gaining that control" (1975, 85). This finding has potentially huge implications for a broader workers' movement across the information field. It shows several things: that unions can play a wider role than a force for mediation, that information workers have recognized the potential of an organized workforce in securing greater control, and that there is indeed a need to fight for that control.

Control over work is achieved on the work floor, not through professional associations that uphold professional principles (such as intellectual freedom, universal access to information, and community engagement) only through current power structures and imbalances, if at all. These power imbalances are often a direct threat to these professional principles and are an important cause of class struggle. Though unions are often labeled as the cause of workplace strife, they are actually the result of pre-existing power imbalances and an organizational tool to adjust these imbalances and amass control

(Hovekamp 1997). The presence of an active, unionized workforce actually defends and broadens professional principles that benefit society as a whole, given that information workers

> often have their own priorities based on what they think is important for their work and organization, whereas management tends to place an emphasis on cost efficiency and quantity. Union organizing is one solution in dealing with this disparity of power, which openly acknowledges the professional practitioners' restricted discretionary powers. Taken from that perspective, unions may also be seen as a means of protecting or even expanding work autonomy and securing a role for the rank-and-file in the determination of resource allocation. (Hovekamp 1997)

It is important to remember, however, that in order for unions to act as a vehicle with which to expand autonomy, the membership of that union must want that outcome and actively strive for it. What is often lost in modern unionism, which is defined by legislated labor practices designed to mediate and arbitrate based on highly restrictive parameters, is the desire for increased workers' autonomy through class struggle. Unions can be the solution that Hovekamp describes, but if information workers want to look beyond collective agreements then they must organize and fight for it.

WHAT IS TO BE DONE?

We have shown that information workers cannot unilaterally assault and bring to a standstill the mechanisms of the contemporary economy in the way that resource and transportation workers of the late 1800s and early 1900s were sometimes able to do. This is due to several factors, including: the overblown characterization of the contemporary economy as built on knowledge and information; the marginalized position of information workers within the wider economy; internal divisions within the ranks of information workers; and a lack of class consciousness even within information workers' unions.

However, this does not mean that information workers cannot be effective participants in wider class struggles. The absolute first step in doing so is to both identify as workers and with other workers of all skill and education levels, in- and outside of the information sector. As Durrani and Smallwood succinctly say, "[i]t is important to understand working people's lives and struggles [and to] be one of them" (2006, 8). What Michener calls the "blueing of the white collar in American librarianship" (1976, 175) is in fact this very process of formulating a class consciousness in tandem with the struggles of all workers.

The class consciousness of an individual information worker is only a seed, a possible node at the heart of subsequent organizing. Therefore, the next step is participating in, inciting, or fomenting organizational preparedness among information workers. This can take any number of shapes and in many North American library and/or archival workplaces, there is already a union presence.[3] It must be stressed, however, that state-certified union representation is not an end but rather a potential means toward greater levels of workers' control. In many circumstances, union representation actually stiffens further struggle as a union run by bureaucrats encourages a service model predicated on mediation between capital and labor, not on direct struggle for control. Therefore, it is necessary for class conscious information workers to actively participate in the day-to-day management of unions where they currently exist, to foster greater union participation among their co-workers, to advocate for radically democratic decision-making within the union, and to use union resources specifically for class struggle.

The mainstream union movement is only one possible means for organizing; the possibilities extend much further and the more we delve into the potential of alternative organizing methods the greater the empowerment and preparedness of individual workers. Organizing can start with simple, rank-and-file, informal workers' groups that form and develop over specific workplace issues, that are fluid and highly adaptable, and that promote the direct participation and active involvement of workers at the point of labor. Such groups would form around activists who already share a class-conscious approach and would work toward strengthening workers' solidarity, encouraging greater participation among co-workers, and promoting a perspective

---

3   Many academic and public service unions, such as the American Federation of State, County and Municipal Employees and the Canadian Union of Public Employees, include library and archives staff.

based on direct action and collectivity. Rank-and-file groups have an added benefit in that they can operate in conjunction with but independent from unions, thereby being a worker-run organization able to hold union administration accountable to the membership as well as acting as a counter-power to management and extant unions.

There are also manifold means of organization beyond the limits of one specific workplace, foremost among these being the revolutionary syndicalist movement as typified by such unions as the North American Industrial Workers of the World (IWW), the Spanish CNT, the Argentine FORA, or the French CNT.[4] These unions form a tradition of class struggle based on solidarity, radical democracy, workers' control, collectivism, and non-hierarchical forms of organization stretching back to the First International. Furthermore, revolutionary syndicalist unions organize across industries and are open to all workers, thus being a way for class-conscious information workers to participate in and link their workplace to wider struggles.

Looking beyond unions and the individual workplace, there are also left-wing affinity groups that are valid options for organizing among information workers. Some of these affinity groups are industry-specific but have a wide or under-developed analysis and are thus open to members from a variety of political affiliations, such as the Progressive Librarians Guild (PLG), which "recognizes that librarians are situated as information workers, communications workers, and education workers, as well as technical workers" and that information work "embod[ies] political value choices" that "PLG members aim to make...explicit, and to draw their political conclusions" (Progressive Librarians Guild 2012). Others are open to workers from any field but maintain a specific analysis based on class struggle, such as the Workers Solidarity Alliance (WSA), which "is an anti-capitalist, anti-authoritarian organization of activists who believe that working people can build a new society and a better world based on the principles of solidarity and self-management" (Workers Solidarity Alliance 2008).

Just as it is important for information workers to first identify as workers, so too is it important for us to reach beyond our narrow sector and build true solidarity by linking our struggles with wider struggles. We cannot build a workers' movement in one sector alone

---

4   For an in-depth study of the syndicalist movement, see Schmidt and van der Walt.

and therefore must follow the example of predecessor organizations and movements such as the Chicago Public Library Union Local 88, which participated in anti-fascist and anti-racist struggles in the 1930s and 1940s (Latham 2008, 29, 32), and the wave of library unionism in the 1960s that was linked to wider social change (Todd 1985, 288). By creating such networks with non-LIS movements, unions, and communities we strengthen the capacity of an entire apparatus of counter-power.

Lastly, we cannot forget the power that we have in our daily efforts and must focus this power toward strategic ends. As information workers, we are uniquely positioned to support wider social struggle in an educational role and as access points to information. Following the lead of organizations such as Radical Reference, which is "dedicated to information activism to foster a more egalitarian society" (Radical Reference 2012), we must bring a class analysis to our workplace, strive toward the de-commodification of information, and use our privileged positions in society to affect meaningful and substantial change, as workers and with workers.

WORKS CITED

Adamic, Louis. 2008. *Dynamite: The Story of Class Violence in America.* Oakland, CA: AK Press.

Adams, Kiely Flanigan. 2012. "The Discursive Construction of Professionalism: An Episteme of the 21st Century." *Ephemera* 12 (3): 327-343.

Anderson, R. N., J. D'Amicantonio, and H. Dubois. 1992. "Labor Unions or Professional Associations: Which Have Our First Loyalty?" *College and Research Libraries* 530: 331-340.

Barbrook, Richard. 2005. "The Hi-Tech Gift Economy." *First Monday* 3 (12).December 2. firstmonday.org/ojs/index.php/fm/article/view/631/552.

Blom, Raimo, Harri Melin and Pasi Pyöriä. 2002. "Social Contradictions in Informational Capitalism: The Case of Finnish Wage Earners and Their Labor Market Situation." *The Information Society* 18: 333-343.

Brecher, Jeremy. 1997. *Strike!* Cambridge, MA: South End Press.

Bureau of Labor Statistics. 2012. *Union Members Summary.* United States Department of Labor, 2012.

Durrani, Shiraz and Elizabeth Smallwood. 2006. "The Professional is Political: Redefining the Social Role of Public Libraries." *Progressive Librarian* 27: 3-22.

Estabrook, Leigh. 1981. "Labor and Librarians: The Divisiveness of Professionalism." *Library Journal* 106 (2): 125-127.

Fine, Ben, Heesang Jeon and Gong. H. Gimm. 2010. "Value is as Value Does: Twixt Knowledge and the World Economy." *Capital & Class* 34 (1): 69-83.

Froehlich, Thomas J. 1998. "Ethical Considerations Regarding Library Nonprofessionals: Competing Perspectives and Values." *Library Trends* 46 (3) 444-467. Academic Search Complete.

Garcha, Rajinder and John C. Phillips. 2001. "US Academic Librarians: Their Involvement in Union Activities." *Library Review* 50 (3): 122-127.

Godin, Benoit. 2008. "The Information Economy: The History of a Concept Through its Measurement, 1949-2005." *History and Technology* 24 (3): 255-287.

Guyton, Theodore Lewis. 1975. *Unionization: The Viewpoint of Librarians.* Chicago: American Library Association.

Hovekamp, Tina Maragou. 1997. "Professional Associations or Unions? A Comparative Look." *Library Trends* 46 (2):229-425. Academic OneFile.

"Information Economy." 2011. *Cambridge Business English Dictionary.* Cambridge: Cambridge University Press. Dictionaries Online.

Jones, Paul. 2010. "Digital Labor in the Academic Context: Challenges for Academic Staff Associations." *Ephemera* 10 (3/4): 537-539. www.ephemerajournal.org/sites/default/files/10-3jones.pdf.

King, Barry. 2010. "On the New Dignity of Labor." *Ephemera* 10 (3/4): 285-302. www.ephemerajournal.org/sites/default/files/10-3king.pdf.

Latham, Joyce M. 2008. "'So Promising of Success': The Role of Local 88 in the Development of the Chicago Public Library, 1937-1952." *Progressive Librarian* 30: 18-37.

Leadbeater, Charles. 1998. "Who Will Own the Knowledge Economy?" *Political Quarterly* 69 (4): 375-386.

Lee, Martyn. 2005. "The Death of Radical Thought: From Dispassionate to Disinterested Professionalism in Intellectual Labor." *International Journal of Medial and Cultural Practices* 1 (1): 23-40.

Lens, Sidney. 2009. *The Labor Wars: From the Molly Maguires to the Sit Downs.* Chicago: Haymarket Books, 2009.

Marshall, James D. 2008. "'Developing' the Self in the Knowledge Economy." *Studies in Philosophy & Education* 27: 149-159.

Michener, Roger. Rev. of. 1976. *Unionization: The Viewpoint of Librarians* by Theodore Lewis Guyton. *The Library Quarterly* 46 (2): 171-175.

Mills, Melanie. 2010. "Information Workers in the Academy: The Case of Librarians and Archivists at the University of Western Ontario." *Ephemera* 10 (3/4): 532-536. www.ephemerajournal. org/sites/default/files/10-3mills.pdf.

Pemberton, Michael J. 1995. "The Information Economy: A Context for Records and Information Management." 29 (3): 54-59. Academic Search Complete.

Progressive Librarians Guild. 2012. "Statement of Purpose." The Progressive Librarians Guild. www.progressivelibrariansguild. org/content/purpose.html.

Radical Reference. 2012. "About Radical Reference." Last modified May 22. radical reference.info/about

Raju, Reggie, Christine Stilwell and Athol Leach. 2006. "The Feasibility of Unionising LIS Workers: A Case Study of the Tertiary Education Sector in South Africa." *South African Journal of Library and Information Science* 72 (3): 208-217.

Schmidt, Michael and Lucien van der Walt. 2009. *Black Flame: The Revolutionary Class Politics of Anarchism and Syndicalism.* Oakland, CA: AK Press.

Todd, Katherine. 1985. "Collective Bargaining and Professional Associations in the Library Field." *The Library Quarterly* 55 (3): 284-299.

Wood, Deanna D. 1999. "Librarians and Unions: Defining and Protecting Professional Values." *Education Libraries* 23 (1): 12-16.

Workers Solidarity Alliance. *Workers Solidarity.* 2008. Workers Solidarity Alliance.

Worman, Anthony and Toni Samek. 2011. "Digital Labor Shortage: A New Divide in Library and Information Studies Education?" *Information, Society and Justice* 4 (2): 71-82. grand-nce.ca/ assets/files/Digital%20labour%20shortage_Tony%20Samek_ Anthony%20Worman.pdf

WORKING WITH INFORMATION: SOME INITIAL ENQUIRIES

Steve Wright

I would prefer not to.[1]

Working with information has become commonplace in the daily routine of employment. Indeed, its very ubiquity within the world of paid work threatens to obscure information's vital function for the ongoing reproduction of what Marx once called 'the present state of things.' For however banal its actual content may be, the circulation of 'objects, such as data and documents, which are referred to as "information" because they are regarded as being informative' (Buckland 1991, 351) has come to play an evermore central role within contemporary capitalist social relations. One of the most dramatic instances can be found within the circuit of finance capital, the lifeblood of which is the worldwide digital flow in real time of particular forms of data. To take just one example, based on figures from the World Federation of Exchanges (n.d., 3): between 2000 and 2009, the total number of trades in equity shares grew by more than 700%, to something like 14 billion per year. Even after allowing that 'the average size of trades ... has dropped 85% over the last ten years,' such statistics hint at the absolutely massive flood of information that needs to be circulated and recorded if financial markets are to continue as an essential moment within the global process of accumulation.

---

1   Melville, 1853.

Undergirding this colossal feat we find the miracle of information and communications technology (ICT), bringing to mind Guido Bianchini's (1990, 171) observation that

> A computer today performs functions analogous to a fifteenth century 'bourg': it is the historically determined capacity to order and channel the flow of commodities, to segment them and compute them.

In what follows, I want to consider information primarily in this sense, as some 'thing' that flows – more and more in digital form – so as to secure the expanded reproduction of capital.[2] This is Michael Buckland's (1991) 'information as thing' on steroids: either explicitly a commodity, or else an input for the further generation of commodities. Such a sense of 'information' will hardly be alien to librarians; it may be especially familiar for those who work in commercial or legal libraries, where it is part of the stock in trade. Then again, information in this sense – the stuff that appears to make the world go round today – is some 'thing' that also exists far beyond the specific realms associated with librarians, archivists, record keepers and other individuals said to specialise in the management of information. It is worth addressing, in other words, because it is precisely this kind of information that is handled in some way by the growing numbers of those who utilise ICT in their employment and are frequently labelled, correctly or otherwise, as 'knowledge' or 'information' workers – even if many of them do so in 'increasingly low-grade jobs that involve repetitive processes of information transfer rather that manipulation or development' (Fleming, Harley & Sewell 2004, 738; see also Böhm & Land, 2012).

There may be other possible meanings of the term information, of course; one obvious place to start in developing an alternative conception is with Ron Day's notion of 'the quality of being informed.' But such a different sensibility, if it is to emerge and become practical, can only do so by first understanding that 'reified and commoditized notion of "information"' which has come to imbue the common sense of the age (Day 2001, 120), along with the vital part that ICT undertakes

---

2   Only when finishing this paper did I come across KjØsen, 2013, which is recommended as an intriguing discussion of the circuit of capital 'understood as a theory of communication.'

in making this possible. This I will attempt to do by reviewing this question from a number of perspectives: through the eyes of those keen for information to serve the goals of profit-making, and via the gaze of those whose priorities are of a rather different order.

CONSTRUCTING THE ARGUMENT THAT INFORMATION AND INFORMATION TECHNOLOGY ARE VITAL TO CAPITAL

> Humanity is in danger of being run over by a steamroller of data (Aly & Roth 2004, 7).

One of the sites in which the 'historically determined capacity' identified by Bianchini has been anticipated and celebrated over the years is the field of management literature. While hardly immune to faddishness, at its best scholarly writing in that arena reveals not only a host of insights into what might be possible when using ICT in the workplace, but above all a glimpse of the hopes that some of its most articulate enthusiasts have pinned upon the contribution of computers to the process of capital accumulation. Back in the late fifties, writing in the *Harvard Business Review*, Leavitt and Whisler (1958, 41) were amongst the first to use the phrase 'information technology,' by which they denoted three intertwined phenomena:

> One includes techniques for processing large amounts of information rapidly, and it is epitomized by the high-speed computer. A second part centers around the application of statistical and mathematical methods to decision-making problems; it is represented by techniques like mathematical programming, and by methodologies like operations research. A third part is in the offing, though its applications have not yet emerged very clearly; it consists of the simulation of higher-order thinking through computer programs.

Some decades would pass – decades characterised in part by considerable workplace unrest – before the use of computing devices became firmly established in offices and factories in the West and elsewhere. When they did, their deployment largely revolved around the first of the phenomena identified by Leavitt and Whisler, with markedly less success being achieved on the other fronts. In the middle of the eighties, two other writers would again use the pages of *Harvard Business Review* to sing the praises of the 'information' in information technology, this time informing their readers as to 'How information gives you competitive advantage.' Presenting their case for the strategic significance of information for value chains in general, and specific commodities in particular, Porter and Millar (1985, 2) reiterated the argument that

> information technology is more than just computers. Today, information technology must be conceived of broadly to encompass the information that businesses create and use as well as a wide spectrum of increasingly convergent and linked technologies that process the information.

At the close of that decade, Shoshana Zuboff's influential work *In the Age of the smart machine* fleshed out this claim by asserting that the use of ICT could enact a fundamental shift in information use within the workplace. This, she held, was based upon the capacity of computers to provide feedback of a quality and intensity never before seen in machinery:

> As information technology is used to reproduce, extend, and improve upon the process of substituting machines for human agency, it simultaneously accomplishes something quite different. The devices that automate by translating information into action also register data about those automated activities, thus generating new streams of information. (Zuboff 1988, 8)

The benefits from the point of view of an organization pursuing capital accumulation were immense: not only the monitoring of all the factors of production in the here and now, but the opportunity finally to realise the second phenomenon identified by Leavitt and Whisler, through the timely provision of meaningful data to support decision making. While Zuboff hoped that such feedback would be available to all levels of staff, enhancing their job control and satisfaction in the process, the reality would see much of ICT's 'informating' potential confined to management layers. Along the way, information and communications technology became intimately implicated in the restructuring of middle management itself (something likewise anticipated by Leavitt and Whisler back in 1958),[3] spawning in turn an extensive sub-genre on the topic within management literature (Dopson & Stewart, 1990).

By contrast, the practical application to business of 'the simulation of higher-order thinking through computer programs' (Leavitt & Whisler 1958, 41) would long seem an impossible dream. On the face of it, that too appears to have changed in recent years, with the growing displacement in certain economic spheres of human discretion by algorithms: most strikingly, in the world of finance, starting with the ICT-driven high frequency trading that accounts for more and more of the world's dealings in securities (Wilkins & Dragos 2013). It is circumstances like this that have lent plausibility to Manuel Castells' claim that information has now become the cornerstone of the contemporary global online economy. As he has pointed out, 'information, in its broadest sense, e.g. as communication of knowledge, has been critical in all societies.' If this is so, isn't talk of 'information society' a tautology? What is distinctive about what Castells (2000, 21) terms our current 'information*al* society' is that

> information generation, processing and transmission become the fundamental sources of productivity and power because of new technological conditions emerging in this historical period.

In the words of Christopher Steiner (2012, 214), author of *Automate: How algorithms came to rule our world*, 'algorithms already have control of your money market funds, your stock, and your retirement funds. They'll soon decide who you talk to on a phone ...'. For some commentators, we are poised on a cusp: the singularity looms before us, but it is capital rather than the Skynet of the *Terminator* movies that threatens to become totally autonomous. What appears, when viewed from one perspective,

---

3   As they then put it, at this level information technology 'promises to eliminate the risk of less than adequate decisions arising from garbled communications, from misconceptions of goals, and from unsatisfactory measurement of partial contributions on the part of dozens of line and staff specialists' – Leavitt & Whisler, 1958, p. 45.

as 'the fantasy of a world innervated by information, ceaselessly mapping and remapping itself' (Toscano 2013), might conceivably be read, from another viewpoint, as capital's latest attempt to realise its age-old desire to free itself once and for all from its dependency upon labour. If so, perhaps Jacques Camatte's (1973) greatest fear of the 'domestication of humanity' by capital will indeed finally become reality, against a backdrop where

> Economic processes are out of control and those who are in a position to influence them now realize that in the face of this they are powerless: they have been completely outmanoeuvered. At the global level, capital's escape is evident in the monetary crisis; overpopulation, pollution and the exhaustion of natural resources.

Does the picture change if viewed through other lenses? Can we learn anything about working with information when examined from a stance that does not accept the pursuit of profit as the final arbiter of all things?

INFORMATION AT WORK: SOME CRITICAL PERSPECTIVES OVER THE PAST FIFTY YEARS

> Information is the most important thing [*l'essenziale*] about labour-power: it is what the worker, by means of constant capital, transmits to the means of production upon the basis of evaluations, measures, elaborations, in order to work [*operare*] upon the object of labour all those changes in form that give it the use value required. The 'disposability' of the worker leads him to be a qualitative indice of socially necessary labour time, by which the 'product' is *valued* as the 'recipient' of a certain quantity of 'information' (Alquati 1975, 113).

In a recent essay on cybernetics, Matteo Pasquinelli (2011) has recalled Romano Alquati's pioneering work of the early sixties, exploring the place of information within capitalist production processes. Engaged together with some Olivetti employees in a project of *conricerca* ('co-research'), Alquati's depiction of that firm was a formative moment for the current of Italian marxism known as *operaismo* (workerism) and its analysis of class composition: that is, the process through which the divisions imposed by capital upon those with nothing to sell but their ability to work might be overcome (Wright 2002). The roots of workerism lie in efforts to understand Italy's so-called economic 'miracle' of industrialisation and urbanisation that followed World War Two. The 'miracle' greatly expanded and reshaped that country's workforce, in the process prompting a massive internal migration from rural South to urban North. *Operaismo* was one response to the incapacity of most sections of the local labour movement – both parties and unions – to understand and engage with these new workers, and with their cultures and needs, so often distant from the sensibilities of the traditional left. Together with other circles, Alquati and his colleagues attempted to map the power relationships within key factories such as Olivetti (a leading manufacturer of various electronic calculating devices), conducting co-research with small groups of worker militants keen to rebuild an antagonistic class presence within industry.[4] According to Sergio Bologna (2001, 12), another of the early workerists,

> In the sixties – co-research, to my mind, is functional to what I'm about to say – we were convinced that within the body of the working class there was already, whole, the knowledge of liberation, the awareness of solidarity, of cohesion, of rebellion. We were convinced that conflict as a form of social identity lay within the genetic inheritance of the working class, but that there was also a memory of hard defeats and therefore, you could say, a 'prudence' that had to be respected.

While Olivetti was then best known for its management's paternalistic personnel practices, much of Alquati's focus was specifically upon the interplay between workers and machines on the shop floor. In this relationship, information was presented as intrinsic to capital's

---

4   Part of Alquati's research concerning Olivetti and its workers is translated in Alquati (1961).

valorisation process, an essential attribute of that labour which is productive of surplus value, in other words of potential profit:

> Everyone in an establishment – even the boss – 'works' in the immediate and petty-bourgeois sense of the word: but productive labour, labour that creates surplus value for the capitalist, must be distinguished by the types of the decisions that the worker makes. 'Productive labour' is defined in the quality of the 'information' elaborated and transmitted by the worker to the 'means of production,' with the mediation of 'constant capital,' in a manner that is ever increasingly [*tendenzialmente*] 'indirect,' yet completely 'socialised' (Alquati 1975, 113).

Like much of Alquati's work, there is a certain ambiguity in this passage. What precisely is the relationship between such 'information' generated by the productive worker, and that value which their efforts likewise bestow upon the commodities created along the way? The quotation that opened this section seems to suggest that the two are identical, although Alquati does nothing to elaborate further in the text in question. Instead he goes on to differentiate between two modes of information. First, as Pasquinelli (2011, 5) also highlights, there is the 'control information' that seeks to monitor and regulate production in pursuit of further accumulation. Second, there is that information 'that constitutes the collective legacy of the working class … 'productive information tout court' (Alquati 1975, 114), which capital through the subsumption of labour attempts to transmogrify into the 'control information' needed for the planning of production. In reviewing management's time and motion practices ('Methods') at Olivetti, Alquati (1975, 130) elaborates further upon the varying forms of this 'living and statistic-ised information':

- • Information in the form of generic and schematic orders, through which the economic policy of the boss is passed down the bureaucratic ladder to the point where the workers take it up within that necessary collaboration with capital that enfolds them. This information of the boss is a correction that synthesises the information leeched [*succhiate*] from the workers.

- Information already accumulated by the bureaucratic apparatus and crystallised in tables etc., together with that accumulated by the Methods department in the mediation of the formal and informal relationships between the various moments of the total worker.

- Information already objectified in methods, techniques, in equipment and in machines as the technical fitout [*attrezzatura*] of labour already mediated by bureaucrats.

- Information at the workers' level, to which the other three sources are also reduced: by mediating the transmission of information circulating in the working class (and in particular between those who work at the machines and those who repair them, modify them, planning others through construction or design etc.), the Methods department leeches information already synthesised by the workers themselves and introduces it into the bureaucratic channel.

In drawing attention to the knowledge that workers impart in the labour process, along with capital's efforts to capture and codify this in some way (whether in the form of documents or of machinery), Alquati reminds us that all information is the outcome of human selection and sense-making, since it is the latter that provides the criteria by which to determine what is and is not 'informative.' What was not so clear fifty years ago, however, was the enormity of the potential leap in command over labour made possible through the systematic application of ICT in the factory or office floor as a means to harness this information to the goal of accumulation. This leap entailed more than simply the mute tyranny of fixed capital: now, thanks to the feedback mechanisms that computers provided, the efforts of employees could be monitored on a scale of which a Frederick Taylor or Henry Ford might only dream. Addressing the matter a generation later from a very different point of view, Zuboff had been hopeful that, unlike the introduction of increasingly automated processes in the factory, which aimed to marginalise the skills and discretion of employees, ICT could be used in the office to enhance workers' capacity to be informed, and so engage *them* likewise in meaningful decision making whilst carrying out their duties. To her mind, this new approach, unlike the mindset demanded for the kind of machine-tending traditionally associated with automated production processes, combinesabstraction, explicit inference, and procedural reasoning. Taken together, these elements make possible a new set of competencies that I call *intellective skills*. (Zuboff 1988, 75-76)

By the mid nineties, Zuboff (1995, 204) was obliged to concede that things had not turned out as she hoped, as corporation after corporation opted to 'automate' their labour processes, rather than risk the threat to managerial authority that the reskilling of staff through 'informating' could bring:

> The successful reinvention of the firm consistent with the demands of an information economy will continue to be tragically limited as long as the principal features of modern work are preserved. Unlocking the promise of an information economy now depends upon dismantling the very same managerial hierarchy that once brought greatness.

A lot of ink has been spilled in the years since, arguing the toss as to the relationship between workers and bosses within computerised labour processes. Amongst other things, some descendants of the *operaisti* have been particularly enthusiastic about what they argue is the potential that ICT offers to those engaged in so-called 'immaterial' labour, in the face of what is deemed to be the parasitic nature of capitalist social relations (Hardt & Negri 2004; Lazzarato n.d.). Others have been rather more sceptical of such claims (Caffentzis 2005; Caffentzis 2011; Henninger 2007; Trott 2007; Wright 2005). Addressing the matter from a different direction, Douglas Noble has questioned the degree to which work with information by means of computers is inherently 'intellective' in the sense that Zuboff used the term:

> In addition to abstracted sense-making, 'intellective' can refer both to (a) the hypothesis-testing and systematic reasoning of the scientist or troubleshooter, and (b) the vigilant concentration, 'attentional commitment' and stress management of the process monitor. This distinction reflects a cavernous hierarchical division of labour along the data interface, a division systematically blurred by Zuboff and others who would conveniently elevate all mental

work, however menial or oppressive, to the level of 'abstract thought.' (Noble 1991, 135)

One of Alquati's conclusions from the Olivetti study was that the workforce there remained profoundly atomised in a political sense, fragmented into a myriad of individual entities, frequently indifferent to any common interests they might share. Much of the success of *operaismo* as a political force in the decade that followed the publication of Alquati's essay was the chord that it struck in many Italian factories where, whatever the significance of their other differences, it was precisely the shared experience of performing tiring and boring work on an assembly line for poor pay that brought together a generation of young migrant 'mass' workers who wanted to do something better with their lives. In the specific case of Olivetti, Alquati (1975, 92-3) would find that through the process of co-research,

> As ferment increased amongst young workers in the factory, and local struggles multiplied, discussion began to address problems of ever greater depth: something that was possible only by returning back to the workers themselves to carry forward the discussion, the objective thread of the thematic's politicisation,

creating in the process the possibility of a virtuous circle open to still further organization and mass struggle against capital. At the same time, many of the *operaisti* would soon discover to their cost that respecting the 'prudence' of which Bologna spoke, and thus taking seriously the old admonishment that 'The emancipation of the workers can only be achieved by the workers themselves,' was often harder to accomplish than first appearances would suggest. While in Italy and in many other countries of the time, the seventies saw many of the practices of social conflict pioneered by mass workers in the factories spread into more and more offices, one of the most prominent obstacles to this circulation of struggles lay in the immensely more intricate divisions that characterised the formal hierarchy within white collar work regimes, where collective effort was directed towards working with information in some form. And if in the years since then, much of manufacturing has been relocated to other parts of the world, service-related 'information work' has continued to expand as a key sector of employment in the West (and increasingly beyond it as well).

Given this, now may also be a good time to return and review critically more of the early studies of office computerisation from the eighties and thereabouts, to see what might usefully be gleaned from them in terms of how employees can best deal today with efforts to subjugate them through information work. Many such texts followed Harry Braverman's influential reading of the mechanisation of office regimes as simply the latest port of call for Taylorist management methods that sought to strip work of its skill (and therefore employees of the potential for job control). Less helpfully, they also often shared Braverman's (1974, 26-7) stated decision to ignore 'the modern working class on the level of its consciousness, organization, or activities,' concentrating instead upon an allegedly objective account of things. One important exception was Rosemary Crompton and Gareth Jones' book *White-Collar Proletariat: Deskilling and Gender in Clerical Work* (1984). Drawing upon their fieldwork in three different kinds of industries within Britain, they concluded that

> Whatever sympathy one might have with Braverman's more general 'deskilling' thesis, it has to be recognised that the 'office proletariat' is not a 'mass,' but stratified by age, qualification and, most particularly, by gender (Crompton & Jones 1984, 210).

Crompton and Jones' findings led them to concur broadly with the notion of deskilling as a reality for the majority of white collar employees in the organisations they examined. In fact, they suggested that the very nature of modern office procedures left it especially vulnerable to 'taylorisation':

> Because clerical work is conducted largely through the medium of paper it is much easier to arrange and rearrange the office and its work station on the basis of the dictates of scientific management (Crompton & Jones 1984, 15-6).

Similarly, many of the interviews which they conducted with white collar workers pointed to the loss of control at the hand of computer systems. In the opinion of one systems analyst they encountered, 'clerks become an extension of the computer' (Crompton & Jones 1984, 55). At the same time, the introduction of new technology in the service of organisational goals could not be read as an unstoppable juggernaut. While reporting that the 'extreme task specialisation' of one firm was 'clearly facilitated by computerisation,' they also noted that 'there was some evidence that the extent of specialisation may be susceptible to managerial discretion' (Crompton & Jones 1984, 51). Perhaps most importantly, however, Crompton and Jones began to question the very meaning of 'skill' implicit in all such talk of 'deskilling' and 'reskilling.' Skill, they argued, was as much a matter of social definition as of technical specification. In other words, the fact that within a specific workplace one job rather than another can be defined as skilled – whatever the actual content of each – had important bearings for the relations of power constructed there. This led Crompton and Jones to the following conclusion:

> although clerical work has been 'deskilled' in a technical sense, this process has not created a homogenous stratum of clerical workers, as Braverman argues. In particular, the impact of the technical 'deskilling' of clerical work has been significantly mediated – for men – by the fact that large bureaucracies such as those we studied are characterised by internal labour markets or job hierarchies, through which individuals with suitable characteristics have historically progressed. (Crompton & Jones 1984, 2)

A number of other analyses written since the pioneering work of Crompton and Jones are also worth re-examining today. Chief amongst these is Ursula Huws' discussion of an emerging class subject she calls the 'cybertariat,' a term used to designate 'the kinds of work which involve telematics' (Huws 2001, 2). In her initial explorations, Huws would look at the question primarily in terms of ICT-based office work – and while this may not exhaust the possibilities of 'information workers' as a category, it does address the great bulk of those engaged in what today is deemed as 'information work.' Examining the class relations in and around office work from a range of angles and prisms, from a traditional Marxist perspective to a Weberian frame of status, and conscious all the while of the hierarchies of ethnicity and gender that are interwoven with those of pay, qualifications, and conditions of employment (starting with the growing proportion of casual and precarious jobs found in offices), Huws nonetheless drew attention to 'an extraordinary and unprecedented convergence' occurring across all but the highest and most professionalised levels of the global labour market:

> From tele-sales staff to typesetters, from indexers to insurance underwriters, from librarians to ledger clerks, from planning inspectors to pattern-cutters, a large and increasing proportion of daily work-time is spent identically: sitting with one hand poised over a keyboard and the other dancing back and forth from keys to mouse. Facing these workers on the screen, framed in pseudo bas-relief, are ugly grey squares labelled, in whatever the local language, 'file,' 'edit,' 'view,' 'tools,' 'format,' 'window' or 'help,' the ghastly spoor of some aesthetically-challenged Microsoft employee of the late 1980s (Huws 2000, 11).

Another key element of convergence that Huws (2001, 18) noted was that of language: 'Entry to the new world of information work is crucially dependent on the ability to understand, speak and write English, or, in some parts of the world, French, Spanish, German, Japanese or Arabic.' Beyond that, workers were connected through the many threads that tie together office workplaces around the world, not the least being patterns of ownership, patronage and trade amongst the firms that dominate the global economy.

One of the least discussed aspects of the ever-increasing application of ICT to white collar work is capital's continued dependence upon labour. However much it may seek to reduce the amount of labour involved in the immediate process of production – indeed, however much it may seek to reduce the amount of labour throughout the circuit of reproduction as a whole, including those (typically office-based) forms of labour directed towards its realisation – capital by its nature continues to rely upon labour time as both its measure and the life-giving elixir that animates it (Marx 1973, 706). Beyond all the debates over the materiality or otherwise of modern labour, over the relationship between production and fictitious capital, over which elements of office work are implicated in the production of surplus value and which in revenue, there remains this simple yet fundamental structural dependence upon labour. Even the apparently autonomous algorithms of high frequency trading are vulnerable on this score, relying as they do upon a host of crassly material infrastructures, and the labour required to construct and maintain them:

> For the costs of financial circulation 'physical conditions' are paramount – as manifested in the fierce competition over co-located server space, proximity to trading venues and access to data, and in related phenomena like the rush to acquire and develop real estate for data centres. (Toscano, 2013)

For this reason alone, it is worth examining some of the attempts to understand, through enquiries and co-research, how those who work with information have experienced and viewed these matters, and what potentialities remain latent within the present.

'FAIL AGAIN. FAIL BETTER': LEARNING FROM THE LIVED PAST AND FROM IMAGINED FUTURES

> To do inquiry is to break with official myths, to be engaged with real people, to ask them questions without knowing beforehand what is supposed to come of it. (Wildcat, 1995)

In the face of the injustices that characterise global society today, premised as it is upon the enforced separation of needs and capacities (Kay & Mott, 1982), should we seek to use information as one means of holding those above us to account? This stance is at the heart of the pamphlet *To Speak Truth To Power* (American Friends Service Committee, 1955), wherein the likes of Bayard Rustin promulgated the ethos of non-violent activism to a new postwar generation. Theodor Adorno (1951) had a rather different take on the merits of such an approach: 'it is true today as in the medieval era, that only fools speak the truth to power.' If we choose to heed Adorno's advice, one useful work to reread today is Neil Postman's *Technopoly: The Surrender of Culture to Technology*. Already a strange and wonderful text when published more than twenty years ago, this book skewers many pretences, beginning with the assertion that the fundamental division in the world is that between those who are information-rich, and those who are information-poor:

> Is it lack of information about how to grow food that keeps millions at starvation levels? ... The fact is, there are very few political, social, and especially personal problems that arise because of insufficient information. (Postman 1992, 60)

And yet information, albeit of a rather different sort to the kind that lubricates capital's valorisation process, is something that is sorely needed if office workers are ever to join with others, waged or unwaged, in moving beyond 'the present state of things' that regulates their daily routine. In this respect, it is instructive to review some of the efforts at co-research in a white collar environment. Two of these, both undertaken in Europe, are of particular note. The first, carried out in the late eighties, involved a study by Italian bank workers of their colleagues' conditions and experiences. This enquiry by San Paolo employees was a significant undertaking, collating the responses to a survey of around 100 questions from 1500 participants. As the organisers themselves wryly put it,

> the satisfaction derived from the success of our initiative and, in particular, from the high response rate, very quickly turned into a sort of panic when we realised that, if we kept to our original game plan, we would now have to classify more than 150,000 individual answers ... keying them into a PC proved to be an exhausting job, worse than any that our own management could have dreamed up ... (Collettivo Credito et al. 1991, 70)

While the survey organisers came from a variety of radical political backgrounds – some active in the mainstream unions, others who had turned their back on such unions due to the latter's moderate policies and practices – they all shared a common commitment to challenging capital's authority in the workplace and beyond. More than this, they also shared a commitment to making sense of office power relations in a time of rapid change, characterised by the growing penetration of ICT into the daily working routine. From this it followed that

> Our enquiry is, before anything else, a political undertaking [*lavoro*] based upon the broadest possible contact between ourselves and other workers, with the aim of establishing or strengthening a relationship of 'reciprocal awareness.' Many questions were formulated in such a way as to provoke moments of reflection amongst those compiling the questionnaire, as a way of 'forcing' us to address problematics – or, more simply, aspects of our own work – that we are not used to reflecting upon. (Collettivo Credito et al. 1991, 4)

In its actual findings, the survey echoed many of the points raised by Crompton and Jones: the hierarchies within the office constructed not only around notions of 'skill,' but also the intimate connections of the former with questions of gender and age. In certain ways, the picture that emerged from the study was rather bleak: despite varying levels of disquiet or disenchantment, the fragmentation of the workforce continued to be its most salient characteristic, and there was certainly no single simple 'demand' that could be identified as a means around which bank workers could organise themselves against their employer.

A decade later, members of the Germany-based collective Kolinko (2002) undertook a project to explore the working conditions and experiences of call centre workers. In certain important respects, this endeavour was quite different from that of the Italian bank workers: in the German case, a deliberate choice was made 'to start working in call centres in order to meet people who work there and to understand what's going on' (Kolinko 2002). Referring explicitly to the earlier experiences of Alquati and other Italian workerists, the Kolinko collective accumulated a host of reflections in the book that arose as one outcome of their efforts. If their means of bringing together their various impressions of the call centre environment seems on occasion less systematic than those evidenced in some other enquiries, nonetheless the picture that emerged from Kolinko's account was one of considerable complexity and fractures within the workforce. At the same time, like Huws, they also underlined the undoubtedly banal, but still powerful affinities that characterise the work routines shared by so many centre employees:

Arrive.

Log into the personnel program.

Start up computer, log into the program.

Start up intranet, check out news, possibly read mail.
Log into the telephone.
Plug in headset.
Switch phone to 'ready' and start.

Talk to customers, talk to superiors, talk to co-workers, make data entries, send mail, fill in forms, take breaks, drink coffee, chat online, flirt, lie, read magazines, find information, have arguments, be bored.

Unplug headset.
Log out of the telephone.
Log out of the software program.
Shut down computer.
Log out of personnel computer.
Leave. (Kolinko 2002)

Are these affinities in routine a sufficient basis from which to begin to challenge the hierarchies of pay, conditions, skill and gender that characterise contemporary offices? The conclusions drawn by Kolinko themselves were tentative at best, allowing some of their critics to doubt the usefulness of enquiries as a form of political engagement (Aufheben 2005). On the other hand, there is much to be learned from Kolinko's admission that their efforts had ultimately ended up raising more questions than they could answer, and that they needed to rethink matters with others before attempting another time to 'fail again. Fail better.'

In terms of a third inspiring 'failure,' there is also much to be learned from the experiences of the journal *Processed World*. From 1981 onwards, its editors attempted to explore the changing face of office work from the point of view of those within a new generation of employees imbued with a 'bad attitude' but no outlet in the workplace for their creativity and verve. While they contained no explicit discussion of the specific techniques of co-research, the pages of the journal remain a rich seam for those who want to mine the ways through which North American office rebels of the eighties attempted to understand and challenge their conditions of labour.[5] Written in a

---

5   Issues of the journal can be found at www.processedworld.com and http://
    www.archive.org/search.php?query=creator%3A%22Processed+Worl
    d+Collective%22; one recent overview of the project is Wright, 2011.

lively and engaging style, *Processed World* brought together not only more conventionally-penned analytical articles on the intrusion of new technologies into traditional white collar hierarchies, but also provided personal insights into office-based conformity and conflict through the form of letters, poems and short stories. Indeed, one of the themes that still resonates powerfully is the group's scepticism around the very meaning of so much of information work in a capitalist society. In our own time, when ecological and financial catastrophe threaten to converge on a global scale, the questions that *Processed World's* editors asked way back in the eighties – what kind of work might be needed in a world where human needs rather than profit have become the priority? – still go unanswered:

> a great deal of work that is today required to keep the system going could be immediately done away with. Whole sectors like banking, insurance, and marketing – the three largest clerical employers – would be unnecessary. Jobs designed merely to supervise and control the population would be eliminated. Millions would be freed to learn and share other tasks, along with the formerly unemployed. (Athanasiou 1981, 22)

Processed World's inability to inspire broader resistance and self-organisation in the office sphere in the manner that its editors had hoped would have a profound impact upon the project. While the journal continued to be published for many years afterwards, the shift from its original workplace-specific focus can be read not only as an acknowledgement of the broadly social nature of class domination, but also as an admission of retreat, however undesired. As some of its editors began to worry, in an increasingly casualised labour market, perhaps the very nature of working with information for capital was enough to drive off those then most likely to challenge authority in the white collar world:

> PW has always distinguished its "take" on workplace organizing from more traditional approaches by pointing out that most work in the modern office is *at best* useless in terms of real human needs, and at worst (as with real-estate, banking, and nuclear and military contracting)

actively destructive. Rebel office workers, sensing this, *don't identify with their work.* They generally change jobs often and work as little as possible. Their revolt takes the form of on-the-job *dis*organizing — absenteeism, disinformation, sabotage. They seldom view as worthwhile either the risk or the effort involved in creating a workers' self-defense organization. Moreover, rightly or wrongly, they believe that most workers, who identify more with their jobs, also identify with management. As a result, the rebels tend to be as alienated from their co-workers as they are from the boss. (Processed World 1985, 2)

In the end, there are no simple short cuts to be had when critically surveying past efforts to promote the collective self-organisation of information workers, let alone raising difficult questions about the necessity of a different social order for the future. In some instances, lessons from a much earlier period may be just as pertinent as those of the past thirty years – in others, if applied uncritically in a very different context to that in which they were originally formulated, past lessons may prove to be of little or no relevance, or even harmful in their effects. The challenges involved cannot be underestimated, above all those of fragmentation and division in the workplace, so that it would be foolish to ignore completely the arguments of those who hold that present work circumstances signal 'little hope … for meaningful "resistance"':

If then, worker's enquiry is about unearthing a secret history of micro-rebellions, exposing the possibilities for struggle in the fine grain of lived experience, and in the process, bringing consciousness of this to oneself as well as other workers, this is worker's enquiry in the cynical mode. We "struggle". We are recalcitrant. But as *techies against business* our struggle and our recalcitrance are integral to the movement of capital, and as *workers against capital* our struggle has absolutely *no* horizon and, indeed, is barely struggle at all. Our day-to-day interest as workers is, in the most part, *practically aligned* with that of this particular capital. If programmers are a vanguard in the enshrinement of use-value, of technological libertarianism, of collaborative work, of moralistic "best-practices", of the freedom of information, it is because all of these things are posited as necessary in the movement of capital. The systematic normativity with which our working practice is shot through is merely a universalisation of capital's own logic. (Endnotes, 2010)

Conversely, one could argue that it is the necessity of 'these things' for accumulation that leaves them potentially vulnerable to disruption by the very workers who carry them out. In most circumstances today, countering capital's directive with Bartelby's choice – 'I would prefer not to' – will likely lead only to the individual information worker's isolation or worse. Find a way to pose this choice as a collective response, however – '*we* would prefer not to' – and the rules of the game themselves begin to change. But what might it take to realise such a shift?

On this score, a last pointer for investigation comes from another realm altogether, that of literary imagination. Although it exists at present only in the pages of fiction, the IWWWW (the 'Webblies') has been evoked in at least two novels as an instrument through which information workers might begin to impose their own agendas upon the terms and conditions of their employment.[6] The latest of these is Cory Doctorow's 2010 novel *For the win* (2010), which features the Webblies attempting to apply lessons learned from the history of the Industrial Workers of the World[7] to a not-long-distant Asia

by signing up people who work in gold farms, which are virtual sweatshops where people perform repetitive virtual tasks, or videogame tasks, to amass videogame wealth that's then sold to rich players. It's set about 10 to 15 years in the future, in the midst of a huge kind of hedge-fund bubble based on virtual goals. (Robinson 2008)

As one of the key figures in the IWWWW reflects early on in the book,

6   The IWWWW first appears as the *Information* Workers of the World Wide Web in Ken Macleod's 2000 novel *Cosmonaut Keep*, whereas in Doctorow's book it is the *Industrial* Workers of the World Wide Web.

7   Talk of the Webblies is more than just a passing nod to the IWW – the 'Wobblies' – which continues to exist more than a century after its foundation (see iww.org).

Gold farmers were easy pickings: working in terrible conditions all over the world, hated by the game-runners and the rich players alike. They already understood about working in teams, they'd already formed their own little guilds – and they were better at using the Internet than their bosses would ever be ... [Once], you'd have to actually get into the factory or at least stand at its gates to talk to workers about signing a union card and demanding better conditions, higher wages and shorter hours. Now you could reach those same people online, from anywhere in the world. Once they were members, they could talk to all the other members, using the same tools. (Doctorow 2010)

Could such an approach be relevant to other information workers, employed in more conventional workplaces than the internet cafes and home environments where gold farmers are typically found? This too is something worth exploring. As Sergio Bologna (2010, 169) has noted, one only needs to make some effort to explore online, in order to discover information workers of all stripes analysing their working conditions:

Whoever wishes to say something meaningful about work has to start off here, has to listen, stay connected to the web for hours and hours and record the tales of lives, the testimonies of women and men about what it means to work today.[8]

Listening to such voices is already a possible first step towards a shared project of enquiry into the conditions of information workers, just as it is a possible first step towards doing something practical about addressing those conditions by comparing notes in spaces outside management's purview:

In their earliest days, at the beginning of the nineteenth century, the first artisans' unions and the first workers' societies were looking for a place to meet, for spaces where a certain number of persons could gather, spaces sufficiently

---

8   One recent example of working in library land is Webster (2013), part of a special issue of *Viewpoint Magazine* on workers' enquiries.

private so that the police and the spies of the companies could record their discourses. It was often the backroom of a pub, a place were a meeting could look as a simple dinner among friends or a gathering for a birthday celebration. Only later, parallel with the consolidation of the process of self-organisation, did it become possible to build facilities, apartments and entire buildings specifically conceived to host the representative structure of the workers, the *union*.[9] Such places became the very symbol of a new power, opposed to the administrative, the ecclesiastic and the financial powers. Today people organise themselves in different ways, in different forms, but this has the same purpose: to create a coalition in order to defend oneself and each other, in order to find solidarity and places of encounter (Bologna 2010, 180-1)

In the meantime, the clock is ticking. As Jason Moore (2014) has pointed out, the ascendancy of capitalism as a global system was traditionally predicated upon access to a fix of 'Four Cheaps' – raw materials, food, energy, labour-power (Moore, 2014) – which are now becoming evermore costly. For his part, in a provocative contribution to the volume *Does Capitalism Have a Future?*, Randall Collins asserts that job losses due to the application of ICT in the workplace are likely to sound the death knell for capitalism no later than the middle of this century. The full force of Collins' case rests upon a ruthlessly technological determinist premise, what he terms capitalism's secular disposition towards the 'technological displacement of labour.' In the past, the mechanisation of agriculture in the primary sector had forced millions from the land, while offering many of them the compensation

---

9   It may be coincidence, but it is intriguing to note that in the original Italian version of his essay, Bologna uses the English word 'Union' rather than the Italian 'sindacato'. As Toni Negri (1970, 442) has noted, 'union' in the latter sense 'is generally understood to mean an association of workers ... predisposed to bargaining the cost of labour-power in the capitalist market. The capitalist determination of the union function is absolutely given: without the capitalist mode of production, there can be no union'. In contrast, the English word 'Union' has commonly meant something rather different, at least in the European radical tradition: a body that, much like the IWW – for example, the Unione Sindacale Italiana in Italy or the Allgemeine Arbeiter-Union in Germany – aims not for 'a fair day's pay for a fair day's work,' but on the contrary to turn the whole world upside down, starting from the point of production.

of work in the factory; subsequent waves of mechanisation and automation had similarly destroyed millions of jobs in secondary industry, even as new employment opportunities were opened in the tertiary sector (typically entailing 'information' work of some kind). By striving through ICT to automate the 'communicative labour' performed by what Collins calls 'the middle class,' the global economy now has nowhere to turn, for there is no quaternary sector worthy of the name that might absorb the latest wave of displaced labour or stave off the associated underconsumptionist crisis: 'Although Information Technology (IT) generates new activities, it does not generate paying jobs at the same rate that it eliminates them' (Collins 2013, 41). Thus, Collins holds, no major new sectors of jobs growth loom on the horizon for white collar employees made redundant by ICT, whether in private employ or in the shrinking public sector labour market of our post-keynesian age. To the contrary, Collins predicts that coming decades will see massive levels of unemployment (and thus social unrest) within the centres of global capitalism:

> Computerization of middle-class labor (since the last decade of the 20th century) is proceeding at a much faster pace than the mechanization of the manual labor force (which took approximately the entire 19th century and three-quarters of the 20th). Technological displacement of middle-class labor is not much more than twenty years old; whereas it took almost 200 years to destroy the working class labor-force. (Collins 2013, 56)

One does not have to agree with Collins' assertion that the working class has been destroyed (since when has 'working class' ever meant simply so-called 'manual' workers?) to concede that his central argument about the impact of ICT upon the labour market nonetheless merits serious attention and debate. Then again, unlike Collins, I believe that there is still much to learn from Marx's value analysis, which locates the potential for a new way of living precisely within the social antagonisms that emerge in response to capital's attempts to commodify human capacities. For even as capital finds itself compelled to reduce the quantity of labour deemed 'necessary' for the reproduction of labour power itself, it simultaneously seeks to subsume ever greater quotients of unpaid labour (both waged and unwaged) to its goal of expanded accumulation (Caffentzis 2005; Moore 2014). In such circumstances, perhaps those who work with information may yet have a singular contribution to make in the construction of those coalitions of 'solidarity and places of encounter' (Bologna 2011, 181) so desperately needed today.

FURTHER READING

Adorno, T. (1951). *Minima Moralia*. http://www.marxists.org/reference/archive/adorno/1951/mm/ch01.htm.

Aly, G. & K. H. Roth. (2004). *The Nazi Census. Identification and Control in the Third Reich*. Philadelphia: Temple University Press.

Alquati, R. (1961). "Organic Composition of Capital and Labor-Power at Olivetti." *Quaderni Rossi* 2. http://viewpointmag.com/2013/09/27/organic-composition-of-capital-and-labor-power-at-olivetti-1961/.

—-. (1975). *Sulla FIAT e Altri Scritti*. Milan: Feltrinelli.

American Friends Service Committee (1955). *Speak Truth to Power*. Philadelphia: American Friends Service Committee.

Athanasiou, T. (1981). "New Information Technology: For What?" *Processed World* 1:15-26.

Aufheben, (2005). "We Have Ways of Making You Talk!" *Aufheben* 13. http://libcom.org/library/we-have-ways-making-you-talk.

Bianchini, G. (1990). *Sul Sindacato e Altri Scritti*. Padua: Edizioni Quaderni del Progetto.

Böhm, S. & C. Land. (2012). "The New 'Hidden Abode': Reflections On Value and Labour in the New Economy." *The Sociological Review* 60 (2): 217–240.

Bologna, S. (2001). "Intervista a Sergio Bologna." In the CD-ROM accompanying G. Borio. Edited by G. Ruggiero and F. Pozzi. (2002). *Futuro Anteriore. Dai "Quaderni Rossi" ai Movimenti Globali: Ricchezze e Limiti Dell'operaismo Italiano*. Rome: DeriveApprodi.

—-. (2007). *Ceti Medi Senza Futuro? Scritti, Appunti Sul Lavoro e Altro*. Rome: DeriveApprodi.

—. (2010). "The Sense of Coalition." In *Post-Fordism and Its Discontents*, edited by G. Kirn. Maastricht: Jan van Eyck Academie.

Buckland, M. (1991) "Information As Thing." *Journal of the American Society of Information Science* 42 (5): 351-360.

Caffentzis, G. (2005). "Immeasurable Value? An Essay On Marx's Legacy." *The Commoner* 10. www.commoner.org. uk/10caffentzis.pdf.

—. (2011). "A Critique of "Cognitive Capitalism."" In *Cognitive Capitalism, Education and Digital Labor*, edited by M. Peters & E. Bulut. New York: Peter Lang.

Camatte, J. (1973). *Against Domestication*. http://www.marxists.org/ archive/camatte/agdom.htm.

Castells, M. (2000). "Introduction to the Information Age." In *Media reader: continuity and transformation*, edited by H. McKay & T. Sullivan. London: Sage.

Collettivo Credito Democrazia Proletaria–Torino, Collettivo Bancari Torinese & Centro Culturale Marxista Mondo Nuovo (1991). *Inchiesta sui Lavoratori Dell'Istituto Bancario San Paolo*. Turin: La Grafica Nuova.

Collins, R. (2013). "The End of Middle-Class Work: No More Escapes." In *Does Capitalism Have a Future?*, by I. Wallerstein et al. Oxford: Oxford University Press.

Crompton, R. & G. Jones. (1984). *White-Collar Proletariat. Deskilling and Gender in Clerical Work*. London: Macmillan.

Day, R. (2001). *The Modern Invention of Information. Discourse, History, and Power*. Carbondale: Southern Illinois University Press.

Doctorow, C. (2010). *For the Win*. London: HarperVoyager.

Dopson, S. & R. Stewart. (1990). "What is Happening to Middle Management?" *British Journal of Management* 1 (1): 3-16.

Endnotes (2010). "Sleep-Workers Enquiry." *Endnotes* 2. http:// endnotes.org.uk/articles/7.

Fleming, P., B. Harley, & G. Sewell. (2004). "A Little Knowledge is a Dangerous Thing: Getting Below the Surface of the Growth of 'Knowledge Work' in Australia." *Work, Employment & Society* 18 (4): 725-747.

Hardt, M. & A. Negri, (2004). *Multitude: War and Democracy in the Age of Empire.* New York: Penguin Press.

Henninger, M. (2007). "Doing the Math: Reflections On the Alleged Obsolescence of the Law of Value Under Post-Fordism." *ephemera* 7 (1): 158-177.

Huws, U. (1999). "Material World: The Myth of the 'Weightless Economy'." *The Socialist Register* 1999: 29-55.

—. (2001). The Making of a Cybertariat? Virtual Work in a Real World. *The Socialist Register* 2001: 1-23.

Kay, G. & J. Mott. (1982). *Political Order and the Law of Labour.* London: Macmillan.

Kjøsen, A. M. (2013). "Human Material in the Communication of Capital." *communication +1* 2 (3). http://scholarworks.umass. edu/cpo/vol2/iss1/3.

Kolinko (2002). *Hotlines–Call Centre | Inquiry | Communism.* http:// libcom.org/library/hotlines-call-centre-inquiry-communism.

Lazzarato, M. (n.d.) "Immaterial Labour." http://www.generation-online.org/c/fcimmateriallabour3.htm.

Macleod, K. (2000). *Cosmonaut Keep.* New York: Tor.

Marx, K. (1976). *Grundrisse.* London: Penguin.

Melville, H. (1853). "Bartelby the Scrivener: A Story of Wall Street." http://www.bartleby.com/129/.

Moore, J. (2014). "The End of Cheap Nature. Or How I Learned to Stop Worrying About 'The' Environment and Love the Crisis of Capitalism." In *Structures of the World Political Economy and the Future of Global Conflict and Cooperation*, edited by C. Suter and C. Chase-Dunn. Berlin: LIT.

Negri, A. (1970). "Sindacato." In *Scienze Politiche* 1, edited by A. Negri. Milan: Feltrinelli.

Noble, D. (1991). "In the Cage with the Smart Machine." *Science as Culture* 2 (1):131-140.

Pasquinelli, M. (2011). "Machinic Capitalism and Network Surplus Value: Notes on the Political Economy of the Turing Machine. *ge.tt/api/1/files/40VrLRa/0/blob?download*

Porter, M. & V. Millar. (1985). "How Information Gives You Competitive Advantage." *Harvard Business Review* July-August:2-13.

Postman, N. (1993). *Technopoly:The Surrender of Culture to Technology.* Vintage: London.

Processed World (1985). "Talking Heads." *Processed World* 15:2.

Robinson, T. (2008). "Interview: Cory Doctorow." A.V. Club. http://www.avclub.com/articles/cory-doctorow,14255/.

Ross, A. (2002). *No-Collar: The Humane Workplace and its Hidden Costs.* New York: Basic Books.

Steiner, C. (2012). *Automate: How Algorithms Came to Rule Our World.* New York: Penguin.

Toscano, A. (2013). Gaming the Plumbing: High-Frequency Trading and the Spaces of Capital. *Mute.* http://www.metamute.org/editorial/articles/gaming-plumbing-high-frequency-trading-and-spaces-capital.

Trott, B. (2007). Immaterial Labour and World Order: An Evaluation of a Thesis. *ephemera* 7 (1):203-232.

Webster, B. (2013). "Notes of a Library Worker." *Viewpoint Magazine* 3. http://viewpointmag.com/2013/09/25/notes-of-a-library-worker/.

Wildcat. (1995). The Renascence of Operaismo. http://www.wildcat-www.de/en/wildcat/64_65/w64opera_en.htm.

Wilkins, I. & Dragos, B. (2013). Destructive Destruction? An Ecological Study of High Frequency Trading. *Mute*. http://www.metamute.org/editorial/articles/destructive-destruction-ecological-study-high-frequency-trading

World Federation of Exchanges (n.d.) "10 Years in Review: 2000-2009." http://www.world-exchanges.org/statistics.

Wright, S. (2002). *Storming Heaven: Class Composition and Struggle in Italian Autonomist Marxism*. Pluto Press: London.

—-. (2005). "Reality Check: Are We Living in an Immaterial World?" In *Underneath the Knowledge Commons*, edited by J. Slater. 34-45. Mute Publishing Ltd, London.

—-. (2011). "Beyond a Bad Attitude? Information Workers and Their Prospects Through the Pages of Processed World." *Journal of Information Ethics* 20 (2):127-156.

Zuboff, S. (1988). *In the Age of the Smart Machine*. New York: Basic Books.

—-. (1995). "The Emperor's New Workplace." *Scientific American* September:202-204.

CRISIS TALK

Toni Samek

> Academic librarians are in a problematic position.
>
> *Stephen E. Bales and Lea Susan Engle*

Author's Note

The Canadian Association of University Teachers (CAUT) Librarians Conference was held in the nation's capital city, Ottawa, October 26-27, 2012. The conference, on the theme "Contested Terrain: Shaping the Future of Academic Librarianship," was marketed in these terms: "Academic librarianship is threatened by Wal-Mart style corporate management that cuts costs by deskilling work, outsourcing professional responsibilities, misusing technology and reducing necessary services and positions. How can our community push back against this destructive agenda?"[1] This book chapter presents key talking points from this author's closing keynote speech at that conference, contextualized in critical commentary about the broader conference activity, as well as a select chronology of important events that have occurred since (up to the time of the submission of this work on 7 March 2013).

---

1   Quoted from the 2012 CAUT Librarians Conference print program.

INTRODUCTION

When academic librarian Kent Weaver (manager of systems operations for information technology services at the University of Toronto Library), accepted the CAUT Academic Librarians' Distinguished Service Award at the 73rd CAUT Council Meeting in Ottawa (November 23-25, 2012), he remarked that in the last three decades:

> Academic libraries and academic librarians have been buffeted by a number of forces, including fiscal restraint, corporatization, downsizing, and a myriad of implications arising out of information technology. Of late there have been a number of studies about the future of research and academic libraries. This has been accompanied by debate and discussion of the "crisis" in academic librarianship. And debate, discussion and twittering about it being a good thing. (2012, personal communication)

This crisis is a symptom of the changing landscape of the academic librarian's parent institution—the university. The current climate in academic librarianship is, in part, reflective of dramatic shifts in the competitive higher education marketplace and how they impact labour through such measures as wage restraint, changes to collective bargaining legislation, and shifting balance between management and labour in a computerized work environment.

In general, this chapter provides for a class based politics in understanding the contested nature of the academy. In particular, this chapter treats the contemporary identity crisis in Canadian academic librarianship. While this is a Canadian contribution to the larger book subject, *Class and Librarianship: Essays at the Intersection of Information, Labor and Capital,* it relates to more universal concerns, including class differences in the workplace, faculty and staff relations at libraries, and the class politics of digital labour.

BACKGROUND

In the 2012 article, "The quiet campus – Where has the dissent gone?", Ken Coates (Canada research chair in regional innovation in the

Johnson-Shoyama Graduate School of Public Policy at the University of Saskatchewan) noted the following:

> Two influences – the shift toward disciplinary priorities and growing engagement with external actors – now dominate the Canadian academy. While Canadian faculty members may chafe a little under the constraints of the current regime, there is an upside to all of this. Canadian universities have gained substantial federal and provincial financial support, and faculty enjoy the second-highest average salaries in the world and enviable working conditions on most campuses. The prestige of the profession appears to have taken a knock in recent years, due largely to the proliferation of campuses and the ubiquity of a university education, but for those who manage to secure a tenure stream job at a Canadian institution the career and professional opportunities are first-rate. ... Some faculty members routinely adjust their research plans to secure funding, be it in the form of government research grants, foundation support or private sector support, but rarely have to accept overt control over their work.

On the downside, Coates observed:

> Canadian campuses have become distressingly quiet. It is not that the universities are without dissenters from all points on political and social spectrums. Many of the country's most radical, creative and outspoken commentators work or study at universities and use the campus as a pulpit. This is how it should be. But the preoccupation with practicalities – work, careers, salaries and the commercialisation of research – has transformed Canadian universities into calm, largely dissent-free places, with the greatest debates often saved for battles between faculty and students and campus administrators. There are no structural or legal impediments to greater engagement. There is nothing stopping students and faculty from speaking out, no grand tribunals determined to impose punishments on those who challenge the *status quo*. We have self-regulated ourselves into near silence, and our

students and the country suffer from the quiet as much as university faculty.

An obvious question, then, for the library community, including faculty, staff and students in library and information (LIS) schools , is: What role do we play in this campus grand narrative?

In Richard J. Cox's 2010 book, *The Demise of the Library School: Personal Reflections on Professional Education in the Modern Corporate University,* he remarked:

> Given the nature and mission of LIS (library and information studies) schools, I wonder just why it appears that we hear so little about such matters of academic freedom in the classroom in these schools. Considering what we teach and what our students are preparing to do, one might guess that the old library school and its successor could be a beehive of controversy. Generally, however, they're pretty quiet. Why is that? (41)

Cox pinpointed a serious problem, one that is key to understanding the present status of the librarian and their labour in the Canadian academic enterprise. In the Canadian context, one cannot complete that understanding without thought to McGill University.

In 2008, CAUT initiated a landmark case, its first case of academic freedom and academic librarianship in the history of Canadian higher education. Kent Weaver and this author were selected as the co-investigators. An important aspect of the investigation and related 75 page report centered on the McGill University academic librarians' (a cohort of 57 people at the time) right and responsibility to teach (moreover to teach freely). The report included a long set of recommendations, many of which are now being taken up at McGill University. CAUT reported in a 26 November 2012 press release that it

> ...has withdrawn consideration of censure of McGill University at its semi-annual governing Council meeting this past weekend. "The decision was taken following a CAUT review of what steps have been taken by the McGill administration to address the series of concerns raised by McGill's academic librarians over the last six years," said

James L. Turk, executive director of CAUT. Turk said CAUT Council was pleased with the administration's actions to resolve the matters at issue. "It has not been an easy process," Turk said. "But McGill's academic librarians have been resolute in insisting on solutions and, with the good will of the university's senior administration and senior library officials, appropriate solutions have been found." (Canadian Association of University Teachers)

During the time of the McGill University case, the 2009 CAUT Biannual Librarians Conference concentrated on several issues, including parity or equity in working conditions between librarians and teaching faculty and amongst librarians working within an institution. As noted on the 2009 CAUT Librarians Conference print program:

> for many academic librarians, academic status remains more myth than reality. Most still trail their faculty colleagues in salary, control over workload, academic freedom protection, and research and teaching opportunities. Progress is being made to close this gap. Associations are negotiating single librarian/faculty salary grids and are achieving convergent collective agreement language for librarians and faculty.

Beginning with the McGill University case and ensuing conference, and consistently since, CAUT has devoted unprecedented attention to academic librarians and librarianship in Canadian higher education. Notably, several CAUT presidents have devoted their *CAUT Bulletin* column to this very subject.

An entry in University of Ottawa librarian Jennifer Dekker's blog captures an important snapshot of hot-button issues. Dekker shared a helpful summary of a former CAUT President's column, "Academic Librarians Are under Attack." Dekker wrote:

> Penni Stewart's article in the Vol. 56 (10) 2009 *CAUT Bulletin* speaks of academic librarians under attack, mentioning deskilling (downgraded, divided into narrow technical areas, work transferred elsewhere), eliminating or freezing jobs, acquiring and preserving disappearing

as an activity (along with its corollary Access), specialized expertise in a subject area being devalued with an accompanying emphasis on generic skills, greater control over everyday decisions, more bureaucracy over librarian activities (and outcomes) with greater oversight of research and scholarly work and even professional development, with an accompanying decrease in academic freedom (2012)

Since Stewart penned that particular column, CAUT has helped McMaster University librarians unionize when they formed the McMaster University Academic Librarians' Association in February 2010. In 2011, the CAUT Librarians' Committee and the CAUT Academic Freedom and Tenure Committee held a joint meeting (where this author was present). In response to McMaster University and its library's treatment of its academic librarians at the 27 May 2011 conference at McMaster University, "The Future of Academic Libraries" (and which excluded McMaster University librarians), CAUT was present and engaged. The activism has endured.

At the 2012 CAUT Librarians Conference, the delegates (who came to Ottawa to represent institutions from across the country) heard opening days talks on: deep structural challenges to librarianship; national library associations and a probing of who actually is speaking for librarians; libraries and librarians under attack, as well as resistance to the assault on public institutions with a case look at Toronto Public Library; and, manifestation of anti-librarian ideology at academic institutions and the progress made by academic staff associations at McGill University and McMaster University in defending their work. Conference delegates then participated in small breakout groups in order to assess the influence of corporatist managerialism in their respective workplaces and to identify means to defend their professional practice. The following brief summaries reflect those group discussions by providing a select sample of issues and tactics raised and documented by participants during the conference and then collated by Erin Patterson (Acadia University).

On an *individual academic librarian* theme, attention was given, but not limited to, the following points: understanding differences between leading and managing; following through with grievances; individual vigilance; keeping up with scholarship and research; exercising academic staff rights more fully; solidarity and building alliances (e.g, with students, retirees); having a voice on university Senates and in faculty or academic staff associations; having strong contract or collective agreement negotiating committees; succession planning for faculty or academic staff association service; and, insisting on transparency in shared governance.

On a *faculty or academic staff association* theme, attention was given, but not limited to, the following points: not waiting passively for staff violations to occur, but rather proactively looking out for them; striking if necessary; forming solidarity with other unions; being active on association committees; having association presidents meet with librarians; offering new librarian orientations designed and delivered by rank and file librarians; educating associations about academic librarianship; having librarians as association presidents; and, understanding the critical importance of properly formed and functioning library councils that are chaired by a librarian and not by a university librarian, though the latter can be a member.

On a *provincial and national associations* theme, attention was given, but not limited to, the following points: the limits of a Canadian Library Association (CLA) membership; creating national specialized library associations; reinvigorating, organizing and flooding CLA committees as guerrilla librarians; supporting existing, and forming new, Canadian chapters of the Progressive Librarians Guild (PLG); having un-conferences, roundtable discussions, separate and new organizations instead of relying on being disappointed by CLA; launching aggressive statements and campaigns like CAUT's "Save Library and Archives Canada (LAC)" campaign; creating advocacy toolkits on websites and access to social media platforms like the Toronto Public Library Workers' Union campaign; establishing a counter to the elite Northern Exposure Leadership Institute (NELI) from a grassroots standpoint; and, addressing the heavy presence of library directors and vendors at association conferences (e.g., CLA) so that academic librarians can have more space to contribute the results of their serious research and scholarship with librarian colleagues.

Following these confabs, which focused on issues of concern and areas of need, the conference delegates heard more speeches on day two. These specific talks were on the subjects of: librarians as teachers, researchers and community members; and, library and information schools and the future of librarianship. Delegates then again broke out into small groups on the afternoon of the second and final day of the conference. This time, they were charged with talking about plans to secure the future of libraries and academic librarianship. Following these deliberations, delegates regrouped for a plenary review about what could be done to move forward constructively. At this point, a structured report back from each sub-cluster on how best to conduct academic librarianship was delivered at a set of microphones. The strategies that were reported fell into the four broad categories identified below. (Again, the examples were raised and documented by participants during the conference and then collated by Erin Patterson (Acadia University)).

On a *funding* theme, attention was given, but not limited to, the following points: undue influence of vendors; lack of transparency in university library budget decisions and perceived misuse of metrics and statistics to justify decisions; too many 'sexy' technology/innovation initiatives without real merit; persistent existence of funds for buildings, but never for staff or collections; and, donations, naming rights, privatization of public space, and prioritization of work determined by funders.

On a *labour terms and conditions* theme, attention was given, but not limited to, the following points: because of more junior/untenured/probationary/sessional/part-time librarians, there are fewer librarians who can speak out without fear; decreasing staff complement, unfilled vacancies, increased workload, so that there is a lack of time to do the research and scholarship required for promotion; erosion of specialists and trend to reduce librarians to "plug and play" generalists; outsourcing of expertise (e.g., patron-driven acquisition); loss of intellectual work; library assistants taking on teaching roles and the blurred boundaries with academic status and/or erosion of academic status; restraints on scope of research and scholarship; and, denial of research leaves.

On a *management practices* theme, attention was given, but not limited to, the following points: diluting the bargaining unit and the turning of bargaining unit positions into administration positions; lack of transparency; indoctrination and grooming for administrative positions; false consultation and imposition of administrative whim/fiat despite "consultation", advisory boards and expertise; over-reliance on surveys as popularity contests to determine priorities; librarians not being on Senate and denial of participation in university governance; misuse of the term 'collegiality' and related concern about the growth of workplace behavior policies; never-ending reorganizations, destabilization and uncertainty; bankrupting of unions, as all money goes to lawyers' fees; divide and conquer strategies between departments, units and unions; and, a customer service mentality.

On a *hiring and promotion policies* theme, attention was given, but not limited to, the following points: fishy hiring practices like appointments vs. actual selection committee processes, as well as problems with the composition of hiring committees; emphasis on headhunters; salary grid placement of new hires at lowest possible levels; generic job postings; making the Master of Library and Information Studies (MLIS) graduate degree preferred rather than required; casualization and fewer (or no) tenure track hires; and, a move to private-sector-like merit systems.

It was directly following this series of reports at the microphones that this author delivered the closing keynote speech, "Defending Academic Librarianship," which was designed to assess the conference's main premise and to point forward for academic librarians and librarianship. So the collective mood already set for the talk was a serious one. Key elements of the closing keynote speech are included below, alongside follow-up points that help bring the discussion up to date at the time of the writing this book chapter in February 2013. To that end, the key talking points are reported in the past tense in order to create a fluid narrative.

TONI SAMEK ON "DEFENDING ACADEMIC LIBRARIANSHIP" (IN TRUNCATED FORM)

As an educator by profession, my approach is motivated by the basic principle that the working conditions of teachers (including academic librarians) are the learning conditions of students. In no small part, the state of the free flow of information and ideas in the global academic enterprise may rest on the extent to which academic freedom parity exists between academic librarians and faculty in respect to collective agreement language, as well as the extent to which librarians elevate the exercise of academic freedom to a central place in the culture of their workplaces, as faculty have done.

Some of what we heard here in Ottawa is a redux of well-travelled terrain harkening back, for example, to the "Academic Librarianship Symposium: A Crisis or An Opportunity" held in Toronto on 18

November 2011.[2] That day was organized around a series of panels and a number of key stakeholders who spoke to specific themes similar to those examined here. The same terrain was re-reduxed, in part, at the 2013 Ontario Confederation of University Faculty Associations Conference "Academia in the Age of Austerity" (January 10-11, 2013), where there was a session titled, "Austerity, the Professoriate and Academic Librarians: International Perspectives," examining the impact of austerity on professors and academic librarians in Canada, the United States and Europe. Session themes included: labour relations, educational quality, and research. Panelists were: Eleanor MacDonald (Department of Political Studies, Queen's University), Jeffrey J. Williams (Professor of English and of Literary and Cultural Studies (Carnegie Mellon University), and William Locke (Head of Learning and Teaching, Higher Education Funding Council for England). What have we learned, relearned and perhaps even unlearned?

On deep structural challenges: If it is true that the gut problem is rooted in shifts in higher education first and academic librarianship second, how will we bring together structural analysis and intercultural or relational analysis to the table? In other words, whither diversity in the ongoing dialogues? Ione T. Damasco and Dracine Hodges note in their article, "Tenure and Promotion Experiences of Academic Librarians of Color," that: "We need to better understand how systemic racial inequities might be embedded within academic libraries" (300). Problematic as they may be, perhaps the new American 2012 "Association for College and Research libraries (ACRL) Diversity Standards: Cultural Competency for Academic Libraries"[3] are a plus on this note. They certainly have emerged as an intersection with the academic library crisis in Canada and the need to probe information technologies and labour interacting with race and gender.

On national associations, outside influences and leadership: This area of discourse is symptomatic of unending schooling in the politics of process and the different cultures of 'leadership.' But to what extent

---

2   A summary of the main themes and discussions were published in *Partnership: the Canadian Journal of Library and Information Practice and Research*, vol. 6, no. 2 (2011).

3   http://www.ala.org/acrl/standards/diversity

have we carried out the kind of 'positive aggression' or 'positive troublemaking' brought to our field by civil rights blazer E.J. Josey?

On threats to public institutions, unionization and mobilization: First a well documented[4] school library crisis over the cutting of teacher librarians in the Canadian K-12 school system and now threats to academic librarians in higher education. We are sister canaries in the coalmine. Have we hit our rock bottoms? Can academic librarians and teacher librarians (and allies) begin to turn the story on its head with respect to a broader library labour movement in the digital age?

On manifestations of anti-librarian ideology at our institutions and progress their associations have made in defending their labour: There is a need to up the ante on ethics, moral agency and solidarity. To what extent is the existence of a national library association, and not a national *librarian* association, an acceptable defense for national neutrality? For example, the CLA has taken a stance *to not* take a position for library workers in library labour disputes on the grounds that it is not a librarians' association. A case in context is the 2011 librarian and archivist strike at the University of Western Ontario. The then CLA President Karen Adams observed:

> In any case of negotiations between institutions and library staff, CLA encourages both sides to work in good faith towards fair and equitable settlements that ensure the on-going provision of quality library services to users. As the Canadian Library Association, we count both libraries and all those who work in libraries as members. We cannot and will not indicate support for one side over another in the case of dispute or strike. Each situation involving negotiations is unique, and must be resolved with respect to local circumstances.

On corporate managerialism: We need to decry the triage approach to humanity, for example by drawing from Catherine Odora Hopper's work, such as, "Renegotiating agency in knowledge production, innovation and Africa's development in the context of the triage society." This 2010 article sought:

---

4   https://clagov.wordpress.com/2012/04/12/cuts-to-school-libraries/

to re-examine the developmental challenges for Africa in the twenty-first century as the continent stands at cross-roads, with bitter memories of its colonial past, and a future she is destined to determine. It is a future in which knowledge has become a key transactional currency. The core argument in the paper is that what matters to Africa is not so much the hype around the knowledge economy or information society and some mad rush into it. Rather, the paper contends that the information revolution that has greater significance for Africa is not a revolution in technology, machinery, techniques, software, or speed, but a revolution in concepts, and thus the way we think about issues" (Hopper 2010, 78-9).

In these terms, to what extent does the academy treat pockets of people as throwaways? Are academic librarians in such a pocket? What are we really shredding in the process of unbundling academic library work?

On academic status: Let's remember the words of William Gibson, quoted in *The Economist*, December 4, 2003: *"The future is already here – it's just not evenly distributed."* Have we tackled faculty librarian parity in terms of a culture of cognitive justice or justice in thinking? Can we better engage an analysis of reciprocal recognition and representation in a time where global citizenship and internationalization are ubiquitous terms in the global educational competitive marketplace?

On library and information (LIS) schools: How often is the teaching and learning in LIS programs reinforcing the notion that hierarchy is normal? To what extent do we teach and learn about imperialism, patriarchy and colonialism within LIS programs? At the 2011 Association for Library and Information Science (ALISE) conference held in San Diego, I was present at a presidential diversity session when then outgoing African American ALISE President Lorna Peterson mentioned something to the effect that: *Well you know what people were saying at the early stages of the I-school movement? That it was white male Directors who were breaking away from library schools.* This gives us pause.

At the end of the day, this is a CAUT conference, so let us work forward to closure from a central CAUT policy, the "Policy Statement on the Nature of Academic Work," which asserts:

Academic work involves both the pursuit of knowledge and its dissemination and application through activities including but not limited to research, teaching, public lectures, conference communications, publications, professional practice, the building of library collections, the provision of mediated access to information, artistic production and performance, and service. All such activities are closely related and involve different aspects of a single job or task. Post-secondary education relies on active engagement in critical enquiry and research, both of which inform the teaching and learning mission of our institutions. The quality of post-secondary education and the experience of students both suffer when critical enquiry and research cannot flourish. The creation of positions that do not involve a range of academic activities in the pursuit of knowledge and its dissemination and application, undermines the mission of a post-secondary institution, which must remain committed to critical enquiry and learning.

Academic staff have the right and the duty to develop and maintain their academic competence and effectiveness, and to perform their academic duties. When determining workload, care must be taken to ensure that the balance among research, teaching and service activities as well as the balance between scheduled and non-scheduled duties affords adequate opportunity for every academic staff member to participate fully in all aspects of academic work. (2010)

The oft mentioned issues we heard about at this conference loop back into this policy language in that they serve to weaken the very concept of the nature of academic librarian work. Let's examine some recent Canadian job postings to reinforce the point.

— *Bilingual Social Science Librarian, Leslie Frost Library, York University, tenure-stream appointment to be filled at the Assistant Librarian level and appropriate for a librarian with up to five years' post-MLIS experience.* This ad contains the following phrasing: "Librarians at York University have academic status and are members of the York University Faculty association bargaining unit ... Candidates sought have "**Willingness** [bold emphasis mine] to undertake university committee work, research, and professional development."

Are we helping or hurting ourselves here; why are we blurring the line around research intentions, especially at a moment in time when we see blurred boundaries of work and leisure in the context of cognitive capitalism.

— *Health Information Network Librarian (Full-time, Contingent Term), University of Calgary.* This ad contains the following phrasing: "Candidates ought to have "An **interest** [bold emphasis mine] in scholarship and professional development and service."

Is this intentionally weak phrasing or simply poor wording?

— *Digital Humanities Librarian (Continuing Appointment), Scott Reference Department, York University Libraries.* This ad contains the following phrasing: "The successful candidate will participate in teaching, reference, collection and liaison activities in the Libraries and elsewhere on campus, and be proactive in developing new programs and services. The chosen candidate will play a role in the ongoing development of information literacy initiatives; participate in special projects, such as assessment, and the development of web-based resources; participate in collegial processes of the Reference Department; serve on committees of the Libraries and of the University; and contribute to librarianship by carrying out professional research and scholarly work. Some evening and weekend work is required. ... Willingness to contribute to the literature through professional development, research, and scholarship."

Note how the purview of scholarship is confined. Would this person's library administration consider an article about digital labour rights as contributing to the literature of librarianship? How would we know? Who decides legitimacy? What role does the Canadian Association of Research Libraries (CARL) play in influence?

— *Digital Initiatives Librarian, University of Northern British Columbia 2 YEAR TERM.* This ad contains the following phrasing: "Librarian members at the Geoffrey R. Weller Library participate in committee work and engage with the professional community through association involvement, professional development, and research and scholarship."

Is the future hire to **engage with** [emphasis mine] people who are researchers or are they themselves understood to be a researcher?

To what extent does the above styled academic status afford academic freedom? Let us examine the "Core Competencies for 21st Century CARL Librarians", section six on Research & Contributions to the Profession. On page nine, the document states:

All CARL librarians should be knowledgeable of, and commit to, ongoing research and professional development through the following:

- Research and publication – contributions through writing, editing, refereeing or reviewing of books, articles or reports

- Conferences – contributions through presentations to professional or scholarly associations/meetings

- Formal study – taken to broaden subject or professional knowledge and may include study for advanced professional and/or related academic qualifications

- Teaching – teaching courses in areas of librarianship, archives or other academic disciplines

- Conference management – planning, organizing or conducting professional programs, workshops, seminars or conferences

- Professional Associations – active participation in professional associations which may include holding executive office, serving on committees, etc.

- Active engagement in community initiatives – especially those associated with their area of professional or subject expertise

- Staying informed – ability to stay abreast of research in a specific area to support a research agenda or to support other work as a librarian within the library

- Research models and methods – knowledge of the fundamentals of qualitative and quantitative research methods including the research process (e.g. question formulation, peer review, etc.)

- Grant writing – knowledge and pursuit of avenues available for grants to facilitate research work

Clearly, we should have concerns about the narrow purview reflected in the phrasings "area of professional or subject expertise" and "research in a specific area to support a research agenda or to support other work as a librarian within the library."Meanwhile, we should pay attention to the Association of Research Libraries (ARL) and its Research Library Leadership Fellows (RLLF) Program, "an executive leadership program designed and sponsored by ARL member libraries that offers an opportunity for development of future senior-level leaders in large research libraries. The program exposes and engages library staff who have the desire and potential for leadership at ARL libraries to themes and institutions that will enhance their preparedness" (2011). Within the multidimensional RLLF Program structure, fellows:

- extend their professional skill and experience base, enabling more effective leadership in a major research library;

- engage the major challenges and pressures currently facing research libraries in concert with some of the major library leaders [unidentified] who are shaping contemporary responses to these challenges;

- better understand the dynamics and politics of campus life in several of the leading research libraries of North America;

- create a network of colleagues to discuss and debate the critical issues and current trends facing research libraries;

- explore the use of innovative and entrepreneurial techniques needed to support the future direction of research libraries; and

- develop a clearer understanding of what it takes to be a successful research library director.

A root question is what kind of leader does "it take" and who does ARL look to (or not) as an exemplary model? To be fair, there are alternatives. Academic librarian Laura Banfield has identified to me, for example, potential alternatives in leadership development, such as the National Library of Medicine/Association of Academic Health Sciences Libraries Leadership Fellows Program.[5] But still, to what extent do CARL Research Competencies in tandem with the ARL Leadership Fellowship foster critical librarians? As Kent Weaver and I were recently musing with respect to emergent copyright officer positions: to what extent are such job ads scripted for "implementation"? Is that what is needed when we consider concerns like the Access Copyright campaign and modernization of Library and Archives Canada? And who is coming into the mix? Who forms the "next gen"?

If the "next gen" is emerging from a Canadian program accredited by the American Library Association (ALA) now, there are but two easily identifiable courses on the books in our LIS schools that deal directly with academic librarianship. These are:

1. University of British Columbia's "LIBR 575 Academic Libraries." This includes a course objective to "be cognizant of professional issues in academic libraries such as faculty status, collaborative lesson planning, unionization, etc."[6]

2. University of Western's "LIS 9630 Academic Libraries." This includes attention to "academic librarian as information specialist, scholar, educator and leader." The course topics include faculty status.[7]

Then there is something different: INF2310H. Special Topics in Information Studies: Rethinking the Library. [8] This might be a good course for Michael Ridley, former CIO at the University of Guelph. He could use this course material to riff off his talk, "Bring It On! Why

5 http://www.aahsl.org/leadershipfellows

6 http://www.slais.ubc.ca/courses/coursdes/libr/libr575.htm

7 http://www.fims.uwo.ca/acad_programs/grad/lis/mlis/Courses/all-mlis-courses/all-mlis-courses_description.htm?UCT=False&TY=0&TN=-1&PI=10&CL=M&RQF=ES9&STF=ES9&RSF=ES9&DF=ES9&CI=-2&CourseTitleId=3576

8 http://www.ischool.utoronto.ca/course-descriptions/inf2310h

the Crisis in Academic Librarianship is the Best Thing Ever," which he delivered in September 2012 for the BC Libraries Group Lecture Series. There he shared information about the innovation boot camp model he brought to Guelph, notably infused with military academic industrial complex phrasings which, no doubt, Henry Giroux would have a field day with. He tells us that he is a big fan of "blowing stuff up." Having been to the International Convention of Slavic Librarians conference on librarianship, human rights and activism in Sarajevo in April 2012, I cannot say that I am a fan of it myself.

Ridley also noted: "We are faculty." "We don't belong in the library anymore." "We need to get out of the library and form our own academic department. We need to get out of the facility that is holding us back." "Every 21st century university deserves an I-school." "The library isn't going away. It will still be an academic support unit." We should "get away from service and embed ourselves in learning and research" (2013). The question I have is: whose research? Who sets the research agenda? If you are working in an LIS school or I-school (and I am), the faculty member sets their own research agenda; it is not determined by administration or CARL (or any other association). You cannot have it both ways.

With a sense of hope and inspiration, Ridley pointed us to the health sciences area of campus, where we see classes of people, adjunct faculty, teaching faculty, practitioner scholars. Does this account for another academic sector where tenure is dwindling? I think CAUT knows the answer.

So how *do* we build institutional resilience? A route forward might be the slow way up through LIS education and into a digital labour movement. Ideally we drive this movement alongside allies (e.g., teacher librarians, public library workers, other public employees). And we elevate the ubiquitous Google vs. librarian debate into a new arena in so doing.

In an article entitled, "Digital labour shortage: A new divide in library and information studies education?" co-author Anthony Worman and I offer preliminary reflection on the degree to which the concept of 'digital labour' appears in current LIS education language, including in course titles, course descriptions, and course content. We also consider to what extent contemporary LIS education provokes critical thought on digital labour and whether or not realities such as library worker unionization, library strikes, and library lockouts, coupled with de-professionalization, deskilling, and the defining, redefining (and even confining) of labour, are apparent in LIS study.

The basis for our scholarship was established from September 2010 to April 2011 through examination of online publicly accessible LIS programs accredited by ALA, the Australian Library and Information Association, LIS programs in South African universities, Chartered Institute of Library and Information Professionals' accredited schools in the United Kingdom, LIS programs in Brazilian universities, and select other programs from the Czech Republic, Hong Kong, Finland, Singapore, and Denmark. Initial key terms used to conduct our search included: digital labour; digital labour movement; digital labour rights; digital economy; NetSlaves; affective labour; digital deskilling; fan labour; digital exploitation; digital volunteerism, and digital divide. A few relevant excerpts are inserted below.

— While not everyone has access to technology or is engaged with it to the same extent, a present industrialized model of higher education characterized by excellence and corporatist efficiency both embraces digital culture and drives its development with a capitalist spirit. Not surprisingly, the field of library and information studies/science (LIS), which reflects its broader educational market, participates in this process of disciplinary decadence (See *Disciplinary Decadence: Living Thought in Trying Times* by Lewis Gordon*)* or fight to struggle and save itself (72).

— To what extent does the current teaching and learning of librarianship produce digital labourers – and what class of them? Can we see markers in the broader geopolitics of knowledge that might suggest our field is reframing through participation in alternative models [e.g., de-westernizing] of higher education? (72).

— Although 13 courses were identified, only one specifically deals with and users rights movement language in its discourse. This is course *MIT 3771F – Net-Work: Labour and Profit on Facebook, Flickr, YouTube and Web 2.0* offered by the University of Western Ontario (Canada). Tags and keywords identified in the syllabus include, but are not limited to: "immaterial labour," "user-generated content," and "Web 2.0," all of which relate to the digitization of labour; and, "the social factory," "bourgeoisie," "division of labour," "(post-) Fordism," and "autonomist Marxism," all of which relate to labour rights/movement. ... Not only does it include in its language many of those terms identified in our initial parameters, but ... the course itself even acknowledges a shift in the types of labour performed as a result of technological advances; the separation of work from place; unwaged, immaterial work; and the de-linking of labour from labour contracts (74-5).

Ultimately, Worman and I suggested a possible emergent paradigm in LIS education that goes against the basic notion of digital labour movement. Our concerns were (and remain) about the extent to which LIS education is preparing its students to gain employment in the digital labour force to simply work in a digital world rather than to effect change by "advocating and negotiating their rights as workers, not to mention those of the people they might administer, manage and mind?" (76). So again ask: what particular scholarship will be produced by the new *Digital Humanities Librarian at York University Libraries?* Will it be projects on digital labour rights, digital deskilling, digital slavery, and technological unemployment? Would those subjects pass the grade for merit?

To close off the conference, can we move bottom up from canary in the coalmine to become a leading player alongside our allies in a broader digital labour movement? In theory we could. In reality, is there enough political will amongst our ranks? Many of us resist management roles–let alone their reframing. Who might recruit and who might be recruited? And why?

Select Post 2012 CAUT Conference Developments (up to the time of the submission of this work on 7 March 2013)

In December 2012, the Canadian Association of Professional Academic Librarians (CAPAL) was launched as a "new, national non-profit membership organization that is being created to promote, advance and support the profession of academic librarianship and to further the professional interests of academic librarians in Canada"

(Barriage 2012). Questions are now in the air about whether or not there is enough critical mass to warrant such an association, the use of the term 'professional' in the name, and the nature of the association's future relationship with CLA, CAUT and PLG. Mike Ridley posted a comment stating, "I do not question the sincerity of those leading this initiative; my concern is with the rationale for CAPAL. ... When I start hearing rhetoric with words like "fighting," "battles," "defending," and "resisting" I get worried. This siege mentality (how wonderfully Canadian) tells us that academic librarianship is up against some form of oppression. I just don't get it. Yes, there are places where academic librarians are not full participants with their faculty colleagues. And yes there have been egregious violations of academic freedom. This is an issue for <u>CAUT</u> and local faculty associations; most of us have been there, done that. If there is an issue, it is in Quebec where academic status for librarians is not common. At any rate, I see all this as something CAUT needs to take up" (2013).

Meanwhile, concern raised in the USA about the American Association of University Professors (AAUP) newly released revision of a joint statement on faculty status of college and university librarians[9] should, and is, raising red flags in Canada. The revised version seems weaker than the original, perhaps especially in its treatment of research and scholarship. Academic librarians' research, for example, is limited to "the discipline and the institution.". Rory Litwin, stateside, posted critical commentary on his Library Juice blog under the entry, "AAUP Backpedals on Faculty Status of Librarians." He wrote:

> [the] Joint Statement on Faculty Status of College and University Librarians" [is a] "new version of a similar statement drafted in 1973 and reaffirmed a couple of times since then. What I'd like to point out is that the new statement backpedals significantly on what it actually says about faculty status. The earlier statement said that AAUP considers academic librarians as faculty across the board, irrespective of how they are considered by their institutions, while the new statement says that faculty status of academic employees should depend upon the librarian's function in

---

9   http://www.aaup.org/report/joint-statement-faculty-status-college-and-university-librarians

teaching, research, and service at a given institution, with the institution being responsible for setting the specific criteria and procedures for according faculty status. In other words, AAUP has retracted its strong support for faculty status of librarians, stating only that, essentially, "librarians should have faculty status where they should have faculty status, according to their institutions." It is pretty toothless now. I also note that there is no link provided to the earlier statement. (2013)At the PLG Edmonton Chapter meeting on 29 January, 2013, a report was given on the placeholder titled, "Anti-NELI Committee," including its development of a "Rise with the Ranks Workshop." Its Statement of Purpose states that:

The Rise with the Ranks Workshop is predicated on the principle that library and information workers should not strive to rise from the ranks but rather rise with the ranks, to paraphrase Eugene Debs. We believe that cooperative, non-hierarchical methods of organization are essential to the social justice ideals embraced by our profession. Therefore, the purpose of the Rise with the Ranks Workshop is to:

- provide a counter to hierarchical, business models of management within the library and information industry;

- equip participants with the skills and tools needed to affect meaningful change within the industry and wider society; and

- foster a specific worker identity among library and information workers;

- build a workers' movement within the library and information industry based on collaboration and solidarity;

- encourage the growth of self-management, egalitarianism, and worker empowerment within the library and information industry.

In context, it was hard not to notice the news stories about Harvard University, below the border. For example, a 12 February 2013 news item by James Cersonsky titled, "Harvard Library Workers Resist Top-Down Restructuring and Austerity," reported that:

the world's wealthiest university is squeezing workers with a new "shared services" model. ... A "shared services" model often entails de-skilling. At a number of universities, converting to a shared-services model for academic departments has detached workers from their localized knowledge and stripped their workplaces of the relationships that help the departments function. ... Under the revamped system, workers face even greater workloads and new forms of micromanagement. Karen O'Brien says that this fall, for the first time in her 25 years at Harvard, managers are receiving notices of employees' "error rates," which, she says, could be a way of weeding out "under-performing" staff. ... The full-time non-managerial staff who remain at the Library make up a quarter of AFSCME Local 3650, the Harvard Union of Clerical and Technical Workers (HUCTW). The union has been <u>without a contract</u> since July 2012, and negotiations are <u>stuck in the mud</u>. According to staff organizer and former clerical worker Carrie Barbash, wages and health care are the main sticking points. Wages would remain largely stagnant under university proposals, and employee health plan contributions would go up—hitting lowest-paid staff the hardest."

Meanwhile, a new book project titled In Solidarity: Academic Librarian Labour Activism and Union Participation in Canada edited by Jennifer Dekker (University of Ottawa) and Mary Kandiuk (York University) is underway with Library Juice Press. The book will have:

a focus on Canada [and] this collection provides a historical and current perspective regarding the unionization of academic librarians, an exploration of some of the major labour issues affecting academic librarians in a certified and non-certified union context, as well as case studies relating to the unionization of academic librarians at selected institutions. Topics [to be] addressed include the history of academic librarian labour organizing in Canada, academic status, academic freedom, leadership in academic staff associations, collective bargaining, and recent attacks on the rights and occupational interests of academic librarians at Canadian universities. The volume includes a broad representation of academic librarian labour activists from across Canada. Little in the way of documentation exists on academic librarian union activism and participation in Canada and this work will contribute to original research in this area. Serving as both history and handbook it will be of interest to librarians and labour historians alike.[10]

CLOSING COMMENTS

Clearly, the telling and un-telling of a crisis in Canadian academic librarianship is ongoing. The potential utility of such accounting and inevitable revisionism, to inform understandings of our national collective memory and intercultural interpretations are yet unknown. But I hope this book chapter, built on the personal-professional traces of a conference speech, will prove of value to academic library and information workers' labour conditions–and of course to the global academic enterprise in which they function and fight for their rights and responsibilities to society and the meaning in their work. Such a worker is Dale Askey, the McMaster University librarian who is being sued by Edwin Mellen Press for a 2010 blog entry, in which he rated the Press as poor quality and poor scholarship. CAUT and the McMaster University Faculty Association Executive "agree that this case represents a serious threat to the freedom of academic librarians to voice their professional judgment and to academic freedom more generally."[11] Many individual librarians and professors and a myriad of groups and associations are speaking up in defense of Askey. A formidable summary by Jake New is found in *The Chronicle of Higher Education* 14 February 2013 entry titled, "Librarians Rally Behind Blogger Sued by Publisher Over Critical Comments." Plainly, this demonstrates how the Canadian academic librarians' crisis transcends the purview of the Canadian campus library. The canary in the coalmine has found its way into the heart of a class clash in librarianship and well beyond.

---

10   http://libraryjuicepress.com/solidarity.php

11   http://www.mcmaster.ca/mufa/AskeyStatementFeb11-13.pdf

WORKS CITED

Adams, Karen. 2011. "[cla] (resend) UWO Libarians & Archivists on strike." Messate to cla@lists.cla.ca. September 16.

Association of Research Libaries. 2011. "ARL Selects Research Library Leadership Fellows for 2011-2012." ARL. January 21.

—-. 2013. "Research Library Leadership Fellows Program." Accessed March 1.

Barriage, Sarah. 2012. "Launch of Canadian Association of Professional Academic Librarians

(CAPL)." Message to LIB Libraries-UAL-Libraries-Sessioals-APOs. December 18.

Canadian Association of University Teachers. 2012. "CAUT Withdraws Consideration of Censure of McGill University." CAUT. November 26.

—-. 2010. "Policy Statement on the Nature of Academic Work." CAUT. February.

Cersonsky, James. 2013. "Harvard Library Workers Resist Top-Down Restructuring and Austerity." LaborNotes. Labor Education and Research. February 12

Coates, Ken. 2012. "The Quiet Campus—Where Has the Dissent Gone?" *University World News*. Higher Education Web. December 9.

Cox, Richard J. 2010. *The Demise of the Library School: Personal Reflections on Professional Education in the Modern Corporate University*. Duluth: Library Juice Press.

Damasco, Ione T., and Dracine Hodges. 2012. "Tenure And Promotion Experiences of Academic Librarians of Color." *College & Research Libraries* 73 (3): 279-301.

Dekker, Jennifer. 2012. "Deconstructing De-Professionalization of Academic Librarianship?" *gone squirrelly* (blog). July 16. gonesquirrelly.blogspot.ca/2012/07/deconstructing-de-professionalization.html.

Hoppers, Catherine Odora. 2010. "Renegotiating Agency in Knowledge Production, Innovation and Africa's Development in the Context of the Triage Society." *Critical Literacies: Theories and Practices* 4 (1): 78-94.

Library Education Working Group and the Building Capacity Subcommittee. "Core Competencies for 21st Century CARL Librarians." CARL. 2010.

Litwin, Rory. 2013. "AAUP Backpedals on Faculty Status of Librarians." *Library Juice*. January 14.

New, Jake. 2013. "Librarians Rally Behind Blogger Sued by Publisher Over Critical Comments." *The Chronicle of Higher Education*. The Chronicle of Higher Education. February 14.

PLG Edmonton Chapter. 2013. "PLG January 29, 2013 Meeting Minutes."

Ridley, Michael. 2012. "Bring It On! Why the Crisis in Academic Librarianship is the Best Thing Ever..." Harbour Centre, Vancouver, British Columbia. September 6.

Ridley, Mike. 2013. "Canadian Association of Professional Academic Librarians (CAPAL: Additional Thoughts." *Exploring the Information Ecology*. WordPress.com. February 4.

Weaver, Kent. 2013. "The CAUT Problem—my speaking notes for CAUT award." Message to Toni Samek. January 29.

Worman, Anthony, and Toni Samek. 2011. "Digital Labour Shortage: A new Divide in Library and Information Studies Education? *Information, Society & Justice* 4 (2): 71-82.

Poverty and the Public Library: How Canadian Public Libraries are Serving the Economically Challenged

Peggy McEachreon and Sarah Barriage

> Like slavery and apartheid, poverty is not natural.
> It is man-made and it can be overcome and eradicated by the
> actions of human beings.
>
> *Nelson Mandela ("In Full")*

Introduction

Public library managers sit in meetings wondering how to increase the number of library users, ponder circulation and program attendance statistics, and try to determine what programs to offer to draw more people into the library. Library staff often wonder how better to advertise and try to broaden publicity for programs. In response, libraries sometimes adopt social media platforms like Twitter and Facebook, at times awkwardly and ineffectively, to try to draw new people in. But does the library community ever address the real barriers to deeper community engagement? The following chapter will explore the issue of the marginalization of the poor in North American culture, specifically in public library settings, and conclude that what is now required are intentional strategies and systematic action by public libraries to develop policies, programs, and spaces for the poor that can have a broad transformative effect on the persistent poverty remaining in North America. Throughout this chapter, we refer to any portion of the population that is facing some kind of financial difficulty, including but not limited to homeless persons, unemployed persons, the underemployed, and other low-income groups, as economically challenged. American scholars often use the term 'poor' to refer to the same populations. In the context of this paper these terms will be used interchangeably, as well as the terms 'economically disadvantaged' and 'low-income earners', though we (the authors) prefer the less stigmatized nature of the label 'economically challenged.'

IDENTIFYING BARRIERS TO INFORMATION ACCESS

Public libraries frequently claim to be user-driven in their service to their communities. Idealistically, these users would include the poorest of the poor–those who depend on free access to the services and collections that public libraries have to offer because they have limited other recourse. In practice, we know that public libraries cater to the middle and upper classes, directly or indirectly ignoring the unique needs of lower-income citizens (Berman 2005a, 53; Campbell 2008, 4; Robertson 2010, 12). As pointed out by Sanford Berman, "[t]he simple truth is that poor people *do not enjoy the same access to library resources and information that people with adequate incomes do*" (Berman 1998, 2). Why does this disparity remain? These authors heartily acknowledge the good intentions, professionalism, and dedication of library staff, managers and board members to provide broad, accessible, and egalitarian library services, as evidenced through the policies established by both the American Library Association (Hunger, Homelessness, and Poverty Taskforce 2007) and the Canadian Library Association (CLA 2008), and yet certain groups of people remain marginalized (Berman 1998, 3).

Public libraries frequently have restrictive policies, both financial and social, that may discourage low-income individuals from using and benefitting from library services and resources (Berman 2005a, 52; Berman 1998, 3; Terrile 2009, 21). Late fees or replacement costs for items can quickly become unwieldy if a book is lost or damaged, and patrons may simply choose not to return to the library if they don't feel able to pay the penalty charges (Holt 2010, 181). Like other government institutions, libraries can often be intimidating and unwelcoming to people not acculturated into 'acceptable' library behaviours (Campbell 2008, 4; Robertson 2010, 12). Many public libraries in Canada are largely government-funded institutions, and therefore, to many library users, the library is another incarnation of 'the man', making it an oppressive rather than a welcoming environment:

> Many poor are at least passively hostile to government bureaucracies. Persons with discretionary income along with health, life and more than minimal auto insurance have an easier time dealing with bureaucracies than those who gain their family medical care in emergency rooms and charity clinics, extend their budgets through obtaining food stamps, pay their rent with housing chits, and have to take unpaid time off work to get auto licenses, pay personal taxes or make court appearances. (Holt 2010, 182-183)

The organizational system (e.g., the Dewey Decimal System) of library contents may be confusing to some people, rendering them unable to access the materials they need as easily as they would prefer — Mellon referred to this as 'inadequate library-use skills' (Mellon 1986, 160). For library users living in poverty, this confusing system may become another barrier for persons already struggling to interact with an intimidating bureaucratic institution (Mellon 1986, 160; Holt 2010, 182). The potential harm here is that people will not get the information they need when they need it because they will not feel confident to seek assistance.

"Library anxiety" (Mellon 1986, 160), a concept introduced by Constance A. Mellon based on her work in an academic library to refer to the intimidation and discomfort people often feel when interacting with the library system, is likely a factor for some people experiencing poverty. People who work in libraries may seem unapproachable because they dress and act differently than patrons with low incomes, or because of the unwelcoming attitudes staff may exhibit, consciously or unconsciously. Diversity employment strategies state that "[p]eople are more easily engaged when they feel represented", and "[w]hen employees are members of the communities that an organization is working in – or working with – it adds to both credibility and trust" (HR Council for the Nonprofit Sector 2015). If university students feel too ashamed to seek assistance in a library (Mellon 1986, 160), isn't it possible that a person of reduced means could also feel this way if they needed to ask for help? What the authors have tried to outline briefly here, is that there are many possible barriers to successful engagement with economically challenged persons that librarians, library workers, and public libraries in general can exhibit and reinforce in their work cultures, and with some of the library policies they create and/or enforce.

As Sanford Berman pointed out in "Classism in the Stacks: Libraries and Poverty," many libraries are failing to live up to the expectations laid out for them in the American Library Association's Policy 61, "Library Services to the Poor." Stemming perhaps from Victorian England and the middle-class ideal of 'rational recreation' (Bailey 1992, 40), the authors suggest that even today individuals belonging to the middle class are seen by public libraries to be the ideal patrons (Campbell 2008, 4; Berman 1998, 3-4; Harris 1975, 2), and as such, library services tend to cater to this demographic. As Bailey described their Victorian counterparts in a by-gone era, today's middle-class are seen as the tutors of the 'lower' classes, modelling more refined manners and a morally superior use of leisure time.

This preference by libraries for more affluent patronage can further be inferred by some of the types of library programs and services offered that seem to be targeted towards these populations. For example, many libraries offer 'gadget clinics' or tutorials focussing on the use of e-books–programs that are largely useless to those who do not own these kinds of expensive 'toys.' The needs of individuals with lower incomes may often be neglected in favour of programs that may draw a larger, or more desirable, crowd or help bolster the image of the library as a technologically savvy place. Homeless persons, for example, are frequently seen as a problem that has to be dealt with in order to enhance the library experience of others – the authors suggest primarily the middle class – rather than as a population that has its own special needs (Campbell 2008, 4; Berman 1998, 3; Terrile 2009, 20).

In 1998, John Buschman wrote:

> I believe there is serious cause for worry in librarianship about our commitment and ability to serve the poor. It is clear that the historical and economic basis of professional

values which has guided an increasing commitment to equity of access is being eroded in the era of the new public philosophy. Our professional response seems to be that we must accommodate it to survive. (26)

Now, fifteen years after Buschman wrote the above quote, what does public librarianship looks like in North America? Is there still reason to be 'worried' (26)? What kind of public library programming is being done in American and Canadian cities today to reach out to economically challenged patrons?

LIBRARY SERVICES FOR THE POOR IN THE UNITED STATES

While much has been written about public library services and programs for the poor by our colleagues in the United States, comparatively little has been written about such services and programs in Canada. For this reason, an overview of the literature pertaining to the United States is included here, followed in the next section by a discussion of the limited literature available about poverty and public libraries in Canada.
   Scholars and practitioners such as Michael Harris and Sanford Berman have long been outspoken on the need to resist libraries' historical elitism (Harris 1975, 9) and to improve public library services for the economically challenged (Berman 1998, 3; Harris 1975, 3). John Gehner has lamented the lack of a consistent progression towards library services for the poor, despite ALA's 1990 adoption of Policy 61 stating, "...[o]verall, the documentation of poverty-focused service remains anecdotal, the province of occasional columns (like this one) and of sporadic comment each year in our journals" (2005, 117). He goes on further to say that "concerted effort... is missing, not only on the part of the library profession but (not surprisingly) of public policy makers as well" (118). Speaking of the United States, Gehner says, "we fail as a profession (and nation) to deliver adequate resources to those who would benefit from them the most" (119). Are Canadian libraries so different? Are we too failing to adequately serve the neediest among us?
   Gehner pulls no punches in his criticism of the general inaction towards eliminating poverty that exists in the US public service. He blames "disagreements about our societal mandate, persistent ideas of "neutrality," conflicting visions of purpose, changes in funding

and support for public services, and perhaps plain laziness" (Gehner 2005, 119) as the possible, and shameful, reasons that proper poverty policies have not been implemented and practically applied in American libraries. Gehner is impressed by the level of coordination he saw amongst public service organizations, including libraries, in Britain to support their economically challenged citizenry. In Britain, this work falls under the umbrella of the Social Exclusion Unit which recognizes poverty as just one outcome among many from the greater issue of powerlessness. Gehner suggests that American libraries take a lesson from Britain: "[W]e need coordinated efforts, grassroots support, a commitment from those who lead, and a closer look at what has been done by our friends across the Atlantic" (120).

In 2006, Glen E. Holt published an overview of the then-current status of library service to the poor in the United States. He concluded that many libraries are still failing to provide adequate services to individuals who are homeless or are otherwise economically challenged. Even when barriers to services for the economically challenged are acknowledged and removed by libraries, the further step of determining and providing additional needed services may not be taken (Holt 2006, 179). Holt underscored a major challenge facing all librarians: the separation between professional ideals/ principles, and actual practice: "[l]ike so many other ALA statements of principle, this one [on library services to the poor] comes to life only when individual libraries deal with the specifics involved in the issue. Without specific thought, appropriate policies and adequate funding, a principle remains a hazy ambivalence" (179). Holt questioned over-reliance on circulation statistics when data on in-house material usage is neither collected nor considered and suggested that economically challenged families may have a strong aversion to increasing their debt and may therefore fear library fines, barring their children from borrowing materials while encouraging them to use library materials in-house (181). To serve these populations, libraries must adapt not only their services, but also their means of evaluating whether their services to these populations are successful.

Holt also asks library workers to critically and honestly re-evaluate if/when library services are offered, libraries are truly dedicated to user-centered service and to reaching every demographic of the public: "Nearly all staff hate to work on weekends, but the reason that stores have Saturday and Sunday hours is because that is when people have time. Maybe your five-day work week in poor neighbourhoods needs to be Wednesday through Sunday" (Holt 2006, 184). If a library truly puts its poor users at the centre of all their planning, these kinds of alternative scheduling options seem logical and appropriate rather than 'outside the box.'Woelfer and Hendry's "Stabilizing Homeless Young People with Information and Place" examines the interactions between homeless youth, centres that provide services to this demographic, the youth's information-seeking behaviour, and how information resources are presented and displayed. The "most significant finding concerned the apparent mismatch between values espoused by the staff and volunteers in the alliance and written in the agencies' mission statements, and the information resources available to homeless young people at the service agencies" (Woelfer and Hendry 2009, 2303). What this article brings to our examination of public library services to economically challenged patrons in Canada is a reminder that sometimes little things, such as how information resources like pamphlets and flyers are displayed, can have a significant impact on persons in an at-risk group like homeless youth. It comes down to accessibility: visually, intellectually, and physically. The fact that something so simple can have a measurable effect on whether or not homeless youth find their way back out of homelessness is significant to acknowledge. Even passive programs and services, if they are truly intended to reach the demographic of economically challenged patrons must be carefully planned and/or re-evaluated in light of the needs and unique information-seeking behaviour of these patrons.

Despite these arguments, the status of library services to the poor may not be as dire as some critics indicate. Library literature is also full of examples of American libraries that have made admirable strides in improving their library's services to the poor through specialized programming. For example, the Omaha Public Library in Nebraska has organized a job fair on multiple occasions in order to help patrons find employment (Bernardi 2005, 322). This library also puts on a 'brown bag lunch' program with representatives from relevant non-profit and government agencies (322) to explore related issues. The book *Poor People and Library Services* contains numerous examples of library services aimed at the economically challenged, including the Read-Aloud program at the Denver Public Library, where storytimes are held at homeless shelters and low-income daycares (Morris 1998,

62), and a program at the Orange County Public Library that provides typical library services to children in an emergency shelter (Carlson 1998, 36).

There are also many programs for the economically challenged that involve partnerships between a public library and other community organizations. For example, the New York Public Library and Brooklyn Public Library have partnered with New York Cares to provide their 'Read-to-Me' program that gives homeless children the opportunity to participate in library storytimes (Terrile 2009, 31); the Jacksonville Public Library developed a partnership with the Jacksonville Transit Authority that provides children with free bus rides to any library location (Haller and Hayes 2005, 327); and the Columbus Metropolitan Library partnered with Children's Hunger Alliance to provide free lunches to children in need at the library throughout the summer (Williams 2005, 321). Learning of these innovative programs being offered in American public libraries inspired the authors in our investigation to find out what kinds of programs are happening in public libraries in Canada.

In addition to anecdotal writings, a number of works have been written in order to help provide some guidelines for those libraries looking to increase their engagement with economically challenged populations. For example, Holt and Holt's *Public Library Services for the Poor: Doing All We Can* offers advice on each stage of planning, developing, and evaluating library services, including an entire chapter devoted to detailing specific library services that can be of benefit to the poor. The ALA's Hunger, Homelessness, and Poverty Task Force has developed a list of ten things libraries can do to better serve their poor patrons. In *Poor People and Library Services*, Sherry Lampman offers a number of suggestions of ways in which libraries can serve the poor through programming. Though it is outside the scope of this chapter to examine these works in detail, we mention them here as possible suggestions for library enthusiasts looking for specific and very practical advice that can be adopted and applied in libraries right away.

The authors' desire to provide a balanced account by looking at both what the critics are saying, as well as mentioning some of the good work that is being done, only highlights the fact that the current level of public library services to the economically disadvantaged do not seem to be enough to have a measurable impact on poverty alleviation.

Yet the critical voices in library literature calling out for better and broader organization among public libraries, and stronger policies and program development are implicitly demanding a commitment to this immense and overwhelming goal. It seems almost unfair to put the burden of poverty alleviation on the shoulders of public libraries, and yet, the critics are asking for it because they must have faith in the ability of public libraries to be leaders in public service to the poor. Are public libraries ready and willing to step into this leadership role?

LITERATURE REVIEW: LIBRARY SERVICES FOR THE POOR IN CANADA

As previously noted, the vast majority of the examples of library programs and services to the poor that the authors were able to find, as well as the guidelines that have been developed to improve such services come from the United States. Although our countries share an active physical border, as well as many other similarities, there do exist many differences in the economic and political landscapes of Canada and its southerly neighbour. While Canada may have more extensive social welfare programs in place to assist those who are economically challenged, it is not immune to the challenge of homelessness and poverty.

In 2008, the CLA issued a position statement on diversity and inclusion that makes mention of library services to the poor. It reads:

> The Canadian Library Association believes that a diverse and pluralistic society is central to our country's identity. Libraries have a responsibility to contribute to a culture that recognizes diversity and fosters social inclusion.
>
> Libraries strive to deliver inclusive service. Canada's libraries recognize and energetically affirm the dignity of those they serve, regardless of heritage, education, beliefs, race, religion, gender, age, sexual orientation, gender identity, physical or mental capabilities, or income.
>
> Libraries understand that an acceptance of differences can place individual and collective values in conflict. Libraries are committed to tolerance and understanding. Libraries act to ensure that people can enjoy services free from any attempt by others to impose values, customs or beliefs. (CLA 2008)

While not as forceful or as explicit in its statement as the American Library Association's Policy 61, the Canadian Library Association has indicated in this statement that service to the poor should be a matter of concern for Canadian libraries.

In response to this statement, one major Canadian initiative launched to improve library services for the poor was the Working Together Project, a multi-phased initiative begun in 2004 by the Vancouver Public Library that focussed on libraries in urban settings (Campbell 2008, 4-5). The goal of the project was "to develop methods for libraries to work with low-income communities through a community development approach" (4). After the project was completed in the libraries that took part in its initial stages, the *Community-Led Libraries Toolkit* was developed and distributed to public libraries across the country to aid them in developing similar local programs. The *Toolkit* includes a number of steps that libraries can take in order to become more inclusive, including community-led program planning, and is specific to the Canadian context. The authors point this out as another possible resource for our readers.

In 2010, Guy Robertson wrote about the experiences of the urban poor in Vancouver, British Columbia and shed light on the value of public libraries to this impoverished demographic. Perhaps as a means of really driving home the truth of poverty and homelessness to librarians, Robertson shares Mike's story: he's an alcoholic, homeless, ex-public and academic library worker, who now survives on welfare cheques and panhandling (2010, 11). Though poverty and low-literacy levels often go hand-in-hand, people like Mike can remind librarians—and all public servants—not to rely on stereotypes. Empathy is not an inappropriate approach to take when providing service in a library. If professionalism truly demands that we abandon our humanity to excel in our career, what kind of success will we actually achieve? Although Robertson drew no conclusions in his brief article, the implication is clear that the economically challenged are often a nearly invisible demographic to librarians. Canadian public libraries need to be reminded to continue to make our programs and services as relevant and valuable as possible.

Earlier in this chapter in the section exploring the library literature examples of public library services to the poor in the United States was a criticism by Glen E. Holt highlighting the sometimes drastic separation between the principles and ideals of libraries, and actual library practice (Holt 2006, 179). This same criticism can be applied to Canadian public library principles. The CLA develops statements outlining values for libraries to uphold, but there are no structurally embedded incentives in place for libraries to take the step to actually adopt and embed these values into their organizations in a measurable way. For example, there is no auditing process demanding that public libraries in Canada prove that they are meeting a set of standards around services for the economically disadvantaged. Public libraries across the country may *choose* to create and uphold policies on diversity and inclusion, but how and to what degree this is lived out in each local library can vary greatly.

As long as public libraries are meeting legislated requirements, and providing adequate proof (such as circulation stats) to maintain their budget allocations from local governments, what incentive do they have to go above and beyond what is minimally required? To whom must public libraries be accountable if there is persistent poverty in the community? As in other public service organizations, managing a public library requires fiscal responsibility, immaculate bookkeeping on expenditures and purchases, the ability to justify large capital expenditures, the development of strong professional networks, and advocacy skills. In other words, it takes significant skill and effort simply to maintain the status quo and keep a public library running. What impetus, beyond a personal driving commitment or passion, is there for a public library to dedicate itself to the overwhelming task of alleviating poverty?

Surveying Canadian Libraries

In an effort to collect some real-world stories from public libraries and librarians who are working with economically challenged populations across Canada, the authors distributed a short survey through email and social media channels. This survey is exploratory and the data qualitative in nature. This survey was not administered systematically and therefore cannot be used to draw any generalizable conclusions from the results. The authors' intent was to collect examples of library services that all library workers can use for reflection on their local libraries' policies, practices, and actions in regard to economically challenged patrons.

Direct contact was made with public libraries in the five most populous cities in each of the ten provinces of Canada by email. The request was that the survey be forwarded on to the most relevant person within the library should our choice of contact not be the person in the position best suited to respond. The authors' desire was to hear from at least one library in each province/territory to provide us with a geographically broad range of perspectives. In total, twelve responses to the survey[1] were received: seven respondents completed the entire survey, and an additional five respondents answered a portion of the survey. Respondents included two libraries in Québec, one from Ontario, two from Saskatchewan, one from Manitoba, and one from New Brunswick. The location from which the other responses originated was not shared.

The first question asked if the library had a priority to serve economically challenged patrons. Only one of the twelve respondents indicated that their library did not prioritize services for the poor. Of those eleven libraries that did prioritize services to the poor, the second question asked if that priority was formal or informal. The authors defined a formal priority as one that was included in the mission statement and/or was explicit in library policies, and an informal priority as one that originated from a group of employees or an individual librarian but was not institutionally documented. Only one library reported a formal commitment to serve this demographic. This formal commitment stemmed from the municipalities' city-wide initiative to serve economically challenged patrons, and involved library programs specifically targeted to this group. All other respondents to the survey stated that their commitment to serving the poor is informal.

Several of the respondents elaborated on their informal commitments. The respondent from Manitoba explained that "[a] mandate of our Outreach unit is to target 'underserved' populations, including low-income," but also stated that their "mandate is very broad in scope and includes serving all citizens. It does not mention [the] economically disadvantaged by name." In Saskatchewan, a branch located in an inner-city community provides services to economically challenged patrons, but in general their library system "serves all residents." Another library in Saskatchewan provides "the same services as most libraries and strive[s] to provide extra care when dealing with patrons with economic challenges such as occasionally

---

1   We are so thankful to the generous and courageous librarians who answered our queries. Out of respect for the respondents who asked to remain anonymous, we will keep all responses anonymous and only reveal the name of the provinces the respondents were from.

forgiving fines." Another respondent from an undisclosed location shared that his/her library works "hard to create a barrier free environment and make sure everyone is welcome."

Respondents were also asked if they believe it is important to develop programs to serve economically challenged patrons. Seven respondents answered yes, while four did not answer at all, and the Ontario respondent indicated neither yes or no, but stated that "[t]hey are a client group that often have enormous challenges to using our services." One of the respondents from Québec wrote: "It is part of the mission of a library: to serve all patrons and make information services and programming accessible to everyone." The other respondent from Québec felt that a focus on serving the poor is important to "contribute to [the] development of citizens." A respondent from Saskatchewan argued that it is important to develop programs for patrons in this economic group because "public libraries are widely used by this demographic–it is often their one-stop-shop." The other respondent from Saskatchewan stated: "The library provides free resources and access to those that may not have an opportunity to attend programs. These programs build skills and provide knowledge [about] their traditional and cultural heritage [for Aboriginal patrons]. The library also provides a safe place to go for neighbourhood youth."

This survey was not meant to be comprehensive, but rather to provide insight into some activities occurring in some of the major cities across the country. The hope was to gather some stories that can inspire an expansion of public library services for economically challenged library patrons in Canada. Further details on specific programs our respondents reported offering to their patrons will be described in the following section.

CANADIAN PUBLIC LIBRARIES AND PROGRAMMING FOR ECONOMICALLY CHALLENGED PATRONS

Seven respondents provided details on programs offered by their libraries for economically disadvantaged library patrons. Respondents were asked: to describe in detail a program, service, or activity they or their library engages in that is specifically aimed at serving persons who are economically challenged in some way; to expound upon the impact that the program/service/activity has had on their community/ target population, and how they have measured this impact; and to indicate any challenges that were faced when developing, promoting, and/or delivering this program/service/activity. Based on the responses we gathered, what kinds of programs are being offered to economically disadvantaged patrons in public libraries across Canada?

QUÉBEC

Some programs and services offered by public libraries in Québec require a fee be paid to participate. These same programs "are offered for free to economically challenged patrons." Librarians "visit community centres and groups that serve economically challenged patrons to provide access to library services on the spot." They also offer "specific kids' programs aimed at and delivered in underprivileged schools." They "offer training workshops" to support adult literacy learners, and "these people are usually economically challenged in some way."

Both respondents from Québec admitted that the impact of their programming has not been evaluated officially, but stated that their "intuition and the comments" gathered from participants suggest that participants gain a sense "of empowerment," improve their skills with "information retrieval," and possibly have "access [to] a better job" when they better themselves. One respondent stated that "We make reading fun, and provide access to programs for economically challenged patrons thereby helping [them] to improve their quality of life." One respondent explained that they rely on "user and community organization feedback, as well as program participation statistics and new library member statistics" to determine whether their programming is successful and having an impact on the community.

When it comes to challenges, these libraries in Québec cited common issues many libraries face: publicizing and funding programs. "Reaching our target audience is always a challenge. How do we make sure our economically challenged patrons (and all of our patrons for that matter) know about the services we have to offer?" One respondent described their greatest challenges as finding "funding to develop programs and hire staff."

SASKATCHEWAN

"We provide free computer access plus one-on-one training when requested. We also fax, at no cost to the patron, job applications and resumes to locations within the city." One of our Saskatchewan respondents described how one of their branch libraries situated in an inner-city community serves their patrons: "This community has a high Aboriginal population, pockets of poor housing, poverty, low literacy, [and] youth and seniors at risk. The branch's programs, collection, and staffing reflect the community it serves. All programs must meet the 3 'Fs': free, fun, and food. The community was consulted on what types of program[s] they want. From this list, numerous Aboriginal-based programs were offered, and the program[s] are extremely popular. For example, the first year the branch held the program, 'How to make pow wow regalia outfits' there were 106 people on the waiting list."

Our Saskatchewan respondents reported that the impact of their programming for economically challenged patrons has been "[v]ery positive. Participants have said [that] a program has changed their lives." Another respondent stated that "[w]e have seen a larger number of patrons come in for computer help but also to have their documents faxed." How have they measured the impact? One respondent stated that it is through "[c]omments staff have received" verbally from patrons; comments "submitted [in written] program evaluations"; "[w]aiting lists for Aboriginal-based programs" indicate high interest in the types of programs they have been offering; the level of "[a]ctivity in the [b]ranch" is an indicator of their success; and "[n]etworking and partnerships with community based organizations and with the Aboriginal community" are also means through which the library can evaluate the impact of their programs and services to their economically challenged patrons. Our other respondent stated that the impact of their programming is "not formally measured — it is observed by front desk staff."

The challenges facing our Saskatchewan respondents include "[f]inding Aboriginal resource people to carry out [the] programs." In addition, "[t]ransportation and childcare is an issue for people to come to the library to participate in a program." Another respondent described the challenge of offering certain free services: "[w]e have to be careful not to impact the operating budget so we cannot fax to long-distance numbers. We are also aware that fines provide some revenue so we do not forgive fines regularly–it is done on a person-by-person basis using our values based service. We strive to do our best everyday."

Ontario

Our respondent from Ontario stated that his/her library partners "with homeless shelters in [the] downtown core" to provide needed services to economically challenged patrons. For example, "street workers regularly visit [the] library to connect with their clients." They also provide outreach services "weekly during summer months, to high needs areas of the city to focus on [the] summer reading club." Another way this respondent's library prioritizes service to economically challenged patrons is through "[p]artnerships with newcomer agencies." The impact of these programs has been measured in a couple of ways. For the "summer outreach [they] took part in a project that measured summer learning loss at one agency," and "[n]ewcomer services are measured regularly through the Federal granting agency." This library also sees the impact of their programs and services: in their "[w]orking relationship with homeless agencies"; because "homeless customers feel they are welcome in the library"; "[s]taff are supported in dealing with issues that arise in the homeless population"; by "[w]orking in high needs areas" which "supports the agencies in stemming summer learning loss in their children"; through "support[ing] their workers in bringing literacy [development techniques] to all their programs"; when "[n]ewcomers see the library as a first point of contact, support network and community link."

This respondent stated that the biggest challenge his/her library faces is the maintenance of community partnerships: "[a]ll these programs are partnered programs that require on-going support and monitoring to [ensure that] all parties understand their roles" and the shared vision of the partnership.

New Brunswick

The New Brunswick respondent shared that his/her public library's services to economically challenged patrons emphasize employment support. "We are doing workshops on how to do a resume for people who are unemployed." The impact of this support has been that "It helps people to get jobs" thereby improving their quality of life. This respondent did not describe how his/her library measures the impact of their programming, nor any challenges they face.

MANITOBA

The respondent from Manitoba described an "[o]ffsite "Check it Out" mobile program" that his/her library delivers "in the lowest income areas of our city. The program offers both literacy based games and activities and a mobile collection of books and magazines for all ages" to use and/or borrow. "There are no overdue fines and staff are liberal in their application of rules including [the] waiving of fines to have users regain library use privileges in the wider library system."The impact this respondent reported is that the library's programs and services have "strengthened community trust in the library," and the library workers have "engaged new readers." They have measured the perceived impact through "[c]ommunity feedback," and "usage statistics."This respondent cited "[l]ack of resources" as a major challenge. With more resources they would be able "to offer [the program] more frequently. The program is limited to 2 afternoons a month at 3 locations." They are also "limited [because] the same staff and resources are also used for senior service sites." Another way the lack of financial resources effects them is that it inhibits them from doing "further research on individuals and families taking part to know if their reading levels increased. [The participants] say so, based on evaluation forms, but that is not as solid a... method of measurement."

DISCUSSION

Judging from the above reports of the twelve survey respondents, Canadian libraries and library workers do care deeply about serving the poorest citizens of our country. Seeing this desire reflected in library policies and mandates would legitimize the work that is being done, as well as aid in the distribution of funding to support research and programming for economically challenged patrons — areas that many of our respondents highlighted as challenges to continuing or expanding on their current services to the economically challenged. The biggest obstacle to making the priority to serve economically disadvantaged library patrons a more explicit and formal priority for Canadian public libraries may be the fear that because the public library is meant to serve all citizens, to focus especially on the poor is somehow to neglect others. As Holt cautions,

One frequent way that governments or professions deal with a problematical population is to marginalize that group. Marginalization frequently occurs when agency leaders determine that what they already are doing for "everybody" meets the needs of a particular population, no matter what conditions that group faces. (2006, 181)

In other words, it may be necessary to specifically target the economically challenged in order to ensure equitable programs and services are actually provided.

Among Holt's recommendations for libraries serving the poor is the need to consider the importance of pleasure as something the library can provide: "Amid these precarious conditions, poor people, just like wealthier folks, have aspirations. They want fun, friends, status, excitement, nice clothes, enjoyable and rewarding activities and respect. Libraries need to furnish activities that go beyond necessity to meet aspirational needs" (2006, 184). It was refreshing to see that of the library workers who responded to our survey, many described not only supporting literacy development and employment skills development, but they also talked about making reading fun, and planning culturally relevant programs for patrons' enjoyment.

When it came to measuring the impact of their programs and services to economically challenged patrons, part of the challenge to having adequate measures is that most of the programs described by our respondents have an informal motivational basis. How can library workers justify putting time, effort, and money into specific impact measurements for programs and services that are not formally mandated in the first place? Yet, "factual analysis and outcomes laid out in advance rather than faith and belief need to be the hallmarks in planning, organizing or delivering library services to the poor" (Holt 2006, 184). Canadian public libraries and librarians do seem to be using the measures available to them to evaluate the success of their programs and services. We can only imagine that the programs and services would improve even further if they were policy mandated, and specifically and thoroughly evaluated for their impact on the targeted population. Though we can see that Canadian public libraries are serving this population, Gehner suggests a need for something more than individual libraries 'doing their best':

Every homework-helper program for grade-schoolers, every English as a Second Language class for new immigrants, and every bookmobile rolling through isolated places potentially meets the need of a poor person. Unfortunately, too often we ignore poverty as something common to these service strategies (and others) or as a concern worth addressing through united deliberation and action. (2005, 117)

Again, it is the incorporation of geographically broad-in-scope mandates about providing service to the poor that could help facilitate the kind of coordination that will continue to improve public service to poor Canadians, and ultimately impact and reduce poverty levels. Public libraries in Canada could take the lead in this matter. They are in a unique position to not only engage on the front lines with economically challenged citizens, but also to be in a position of power and influence with public policy-makers and governing decision-makers.

Conclusion

The wrong library question that many public libraries might ask
at this point is
"What services should my library offer to the poor?"
The right question is more complex:
"How can my library develop and fit its services into the lives
of the poor so they will benefit from what we know how to do"?

Glen Holt (2006, 184)

There is no question that public libraries need to strategically plan their programs, collections, and services to meet the needs of many segments of society, including those in the middle class. Public libraries also need to be accountable to their municipalities and other sources of funding for fiscally responsible spending and efficient use of library materials and assets. However, it is vital that librarians not hide behind policies that may inadvertently exclude people with low incomes, claiming that it is necessary for the proper functioning of the library. The alternative is to embrace the responsibility that comes with power, and to commit to serving those who most desperately need access to the services the library has to offer.

The recent phenomenon of the Occupy libraries that sprang up within Occupy communities in various American and Canadian cities and towns was a wake-up call for many. In what ways are libraries failing to meet the needs of a sizable portion of the population? Perhaps the better question is, do libraries need to stop claiming that they can serve everyone and start focusing on serving those with the greatest need? Interestingly, librarians like John Pateman who engage in evidence-based research on the subject suggest that it is *only* by focusing efforts on the most marginalized populations that libraries can actually achieve their claim and serve everyone adequately. In his presentation at the 2014 Atlantic Provinces Library Association (APLA) conference, Pateman displayed a circular diagram to illustrate his argument that when library services (or any publicly funded social services for that matter) focus to reach those on the fringes (the outer edges of the circle), the needs of everyone else on the inside is met by default. In other words, he put to rest any fears that choosing to focus library services on the economically challenged means abandoning our loyal middle-class patrons of times past for they too will benefit.

The analogy of accessibility design can further help to illustrate this: when a new building is designed to meet wheelchair accessibility standards for example, the result actually benefits a much broader range of people than only those in wheelchairs – automatic doors can help the person who's arms are full carrying bulky packages, or who is too small or weak to push open a heavy door. Similarly, a ramp may be easier for a person on crutches or who uses a cane to ascend rather than stairs. Pateman argues that a fundamental shift in how public libraries in Canada operate will have a beneficial impact – he refers to this as a move towards "community-led" public libraries (for more on this see his co-authored book *Developing Community-Led Public Libraries: Evidence from the UK and Canada* by John Pateman and Ken Williment, 2013).

Many librarians wonder how libraries can remain relevant in a rapidly changing world. The responses we received from public libraries in a variety of Canadian provinces indicate to these authors that libraries are on the right track. Canadian public libraries are taking seriously the issue of serving the needs of economically challenged citizens as is evidenced by the programs described. Now is not the time to stop. It's clear what needs to be done – when libraries make a deeper commitment to serving the economically challenged they will not simply be following their hearts. Researchers like Pateman and Williment continue to collect data to prove that this focus has a strong evidence-base as the most effective means forward. Librarians and library staff have the knowledge, experience, resources, skills and passion needed. The question is do they have the courage and the drive to make services to the poor the number one priority for public libraries? The opportunity exists for each one of us to contribute to the betterment of our communities, and our country in this way. We're in. Are you?

WORKS CITED

Bailey, Peter. 1992. "Leisure and Class in Victorian England." In *Reading Into Cultural Studies*, edited by Martin Barker and Anne Beezer, 34-48. New York: Routledge.

Berman, Sanford. 2005. "Classism in the Stacks: Libraries and Poor People." *Librarians at Liberty* 13 (3): 51-54. Counterpoise.

—-. 2005. "Classism in the Stacks: Libraries and Poverty." *Journal of Information Ethics* 16 (1): 103-110. Library Literature and Information Science Full Text. doi:10.3172/JIE.16.1.103.

—-. 1998. "Foreword". In *Poor People and Library Services*, edited by Karen M. Venturella, 1-14. Jefferson, NC: McFarland.

Bernardi, John. 2005. "The Poor and the Public Library." *Public Libraries* 44 (6): 321-323. Library   Literature and Information Science Full Text.

Buschman, John. 1998. "History and Theory of Information Poverty." In *Poor People and Library Services*, edited by Karen M. Venturella, 16-28. Jefferson, NC: McFarland.

Campbell, Brian. 2008. "Why Working Together." Preface. *Community-Led Libraries Toolkit*, by Working Together Project, 4-6. Vancouver: Working Together Project. www.librariesincommunities.ca/resources/Community-Led_Libraries_Toolkit.pdf.

Canadian Library Association. 2008. "Canadian Library Association / Association canadienne des bibliothèques Position Statement on Diversity and Inclusion." Canadian Library Association,. May 25.

Carlson, Pam. 1998. "'Reading Can Give You a Dream'." In *Poor People and Library Services*, edited by Karen M. Venturella, 36-43. Jefferson, NC: McFarland.

Gehner, John. 2005. "Poverty, Poor People, and Our Priorities." *Reference & User Services Quarterly* 45 (2): 117-121. Library Literature and Information Science Full Text.

Haller, Anita, and Keith Hayes. 2005. "Jacksonville Public Library Service to Low-Income Urban Areas." *Public Libraries* 44 (6): 327-328. Library Literature and Information Science Full Text.

Harris, Michael H. 1975. "The Role of the Public Library in American Life: A Speculative Essay." In *Occasional Papers* 117, 1-42. [Champaign]: University of Illinois, Graduate School of Library Science.

Holt, Glen E. 2006. "Fitting Library Services into the Lives of the Poor." *The Bottom Line: Managing Library Finances* 19 (1): 179-186. Library Literature and Information Science Full Text. doi:10.1108/08880450610713063.

Holt, Leslie Edmonds and Glen E. Holt. 2010. *Public Library Services for the Poor: Doing All We Can.* Chicago: American Library Association.

HR Council for the Nonprofit Sector. 2015. "Diversity at Work: Why a Diverse Workplace Matters." Community Foundations of Canada. Accessed April 18. hrcouncil.ca/hr-toolkit/diversity-workforce-matters.cfm.

Hunger, Homelessness, and Poverty Task Force. 2007. "Ten Things You Can Work on to Better Serve Low Income People in Your Library." Social Responsibilities Round Table of the American Library Association. hhptf.org/article/378/ten-things-you-can-work-on-to-better-serve-low-income-people-in-your-library.

BBC News. 2005. "In Full: Mandela's Poverty Speech." BBC. February 3.

Lampman, Sherry. 1998. "Ways to Make a Difference." In *Poor People and Library Services*, edited by Karen M. Venturella, 118-22. Jefferson, NC: McFarland.

Mellon, Constance A. 1986. "Library Anxiety: A Grounded Theory and Its Development." *College & Research Libraries* 47 (2): 160-165.

Morris, Sharon. 1998. "Denver Public Library Reads Aloud to Young Children." In *Poor People and Library Services*, edited by Karen M. Venturella, 62-69. Jefferson, NC: McFarland.

Pateman, John. 2014. "Developing a Community-Led Public Library." Paper presented at the Atlantic Provinces Library Association Conference, Moncton, NB, June 4.

Robertson, Guy. 2010. "What Goes Down: Library Experiences of the Urban Poor." *Feliciter* 56 (1): 10-12. Library & Information Science Source.

Terrile, Vikki C. 2009. "Library Services to Children, Teens and Families Experiencing Homelessness." *Urban Library Journal* 15(2): 21-34. Library Literature and Information Science Full Text.

Venturella, Karen M., ed. 1998. *Poor People and Library Services*. Jefferson, NC: McFarland.

Williams, Cathy. 2005. "Serving Urban Populations." *Public Libraries* 44 (6): 320-321. Library Literature and Information Science Full Text.

Woelfer, Jill Palzkill and David G. Hendry. 2009. "Stabilizing Homeless Young People with Information and Place." *Journal of the American Society for Information Science and Technology* 60 (11):2300-12. Library Literature and Information Science Full Text. doi:10.1002/asi.21146.

Lost in the Gaps: The Plight of the *Pro Se* Patron

Carey Sias

Access to justice is a basic right to American litigants, but a growing number of low-income and vulnerable people are forced to advocate for themselves in legal matters because they cannot afford to hire an attorney. These unrepresented parties are often referred to as proceeding *pro se*, or as "self represented litigants," hereinafter "SRLs." Services are available for some low-income populations, but legal aid organizations lack sufficient resources to keep up with public demand. Less than one in five low-income and indigent people with civil legal problems are represented by pro bono, paid, or legal aid attorneys, in part due to rising costs of legal services and decreases in legal aid funding. Economic limitations force legal programs for low-income populations to turn away about half of the eligible clients seeking services every year (Legal Services Corporation (hereinafter "LSC") 2009, 1-2).

Although the right to appointed counsel in criminal cases is long-established, the U.S. government recognizes that "[i]nequalities remain … because neither the U.S. Constitution or federal statutes provide a right to government-appointed counsel in civil cases when individuals are unable to afford it" (United States 2011, sec. 301). Unrepresented parties are particularly disadvantaged in cases involving basic needs such as housing, family law, social security, unemployment, and immigration (Columbia Law School Human Rights Clinic (hereinafter "Columbia") 2014, 412), and in cases where the other party has a lawyer. Federal U.S government initiatives address issues of legal inequality but are insufficient to close the justice gap.

All litigants are held to the same standards, whether or not they are represented by counsel. Most SRLs have a relative lack of legal education and courtroom experience, inhibiting their abilities to participate effectively in their own cases. The American justice system is not uniform, and procedures vary by jurisdiction, court, and judge (National Center for State Courts (hereinafter "NCSC"), 9). Few courts or law libraries offer self-help centers. The complexity of navigating court systems increases the likelihood of negative and unjust outcomes for SRL litigants and also places a burden on the court itself (LSC 2009, 23).

Public law libraries are in a position to help bridge the justice gap by providing neutral access to legal information, regardless of patron income or legal qualifications. The American Association of Law Libraries (AALL) has "an obligation to satisfy the needs, to promote the interests and to respect the values of their clientele," and supports the concept of access to justice through "open access to information for all individuals," including the general public (1999). Although law librarians are ethically unauthorized to interpret the law or provide direct representation, they do facilitate information distribution through maintaining library collections and internet resources, which might be the only source of legal information available to SRLs. Many law libraries are seeing a dramatic increase of SRL and public patrons, even as visits by lawyers and court staff decrease (Zorza 2012, 1). Public law librarians around the country recognize growing legal needs in their communities and are developing services such as document assembly programs, plain-language forms, referrals, and self-help programs specifically for SRL patrons.

Law libraries have potential to make the judicial system more accessible and user-friendly to the growing SRL patron base through a combination of in-person and online services, involvement in justice initiatives, and collaboration with courts and legal aid organizations. This essay will review key studies and recent literature to explore the current landscape and obstacles facing self-represented litigants who seek civil legal assistance, identify where certain federal legal aid initiatives fall short in fulfilling the U.S. responsibility to provide equality, and consider ways in which law libraries can and do play a role in ensuring greater access to justice.

Legal Aid Services and Self-Represented Litigants

As of this writing, no national resource compiles statistics on the total number of SRLs in all county, state, and federal courts. LSC-funded legal service providers are the primary source of aid for low-income Americans (LSC 2009, 19-20). Utilizing data provided by surveys and affiliated legal aid programs, LSC published the groundbreaking *Documenting the Justice Gap In America* report in 2005, and issued an updated report in 2009 to illustrate the growing justice gap in America (23-27). Both reports indicate that less than one in five low-income people obtain legal assistance or representation from an attorney, and limited resources compel LSC programs to reject half of the eligible clients seeking legal assistance (1). About one million people each year are turned away (9). These findings do not account for people with legal needs who do not ask for LSC assistance, clients seeking help from non-LSC funded programs, or those who do not meet the income eligibility criteria.

The 2009 *Documenting the Justice Gap* report shows a particular increase of SRLs in family and housing courts, with judges reporting a notable difference between 2008 and 2009 (LSC 2009, 26-27). LSC identifies the rise related to "[t]he current economic crisis, with its attendant problems of high unemployment, home foreclosures and family stress, has resulted in legal problems relating to consumer credit, housing, employment, bankruptcies, domestic violence and child support, and has pushed many families into poverty for the first time" (5). Many of these cases involve crisis situations regarding basic human needs.

Eligibility requirements for clients seeking assistance from any LSC-affiliated legal aid organization specify a maximum income level of 125% of the federal poverty guidelines (LSC 2009, 7). At the time of the first *Justice Gap* report in 2005, 49.6 million citizens qualified for legal aid; by the time the 2009 report was published that number had grown to 53.8 million (6). As of 2013, 60.2 million Americans meet the economic qualification for LSC services (DeNavas-Walt & Proctor 2014, 6). The median household income in America has fallen 8% between 2007 and 2013. Income levels are lower for Hispanic and black families, single women, immigrants, and those living outside metropolitan areas (5); these are typically populations in dire need of legal assistance.

At the same time, funding for legal services has decreased dramatically. Annual appropriations for LSC organizations have steadily dropped since 2010 (LSC 2014, 3) in part due to declining legal aid funding revenues from IOLTA interest rates (Columbia 2014, 422). The crisis in unmet civil legal needs disproportionately affects low-income and poor people, women, minorities, immigrants, and non-English speakers (410-414). Many middle-class Americans are also priced out of the legal system when they exceed maximum income requirements for legal aid but cannot afford attorney representation.

A right to counsel is guaranteed for most criminal defendants in U.S. state and federal courts under the Sixth Amendment and landmark U.S. Supreme Court cases such as *Gideon v. Wainwright* (National Legal Aid 2011). The Human Rights Committee has established protections that include the right to free legal aid in civil cases, but the U.S government does not currently recognize these obligations (Columbia 2014, 416-420). In a 2001 report to the U.N. Committee on Human Rights, the United States admitted that "[i] nequalities remain [...] because neither the U.S. Constitution nor federal statutes provide a right to government-appointed counsel in civil cases when individuals are unable to afford it" (United States 2011, sec. 301). This is especially problematic in immigration courts, where 84% of detained noncitizens lack counsel to advocate for basic human needs on their behalf (Columbia 2014, 414).

FEDERAL JUSTICE INITIATIVES: LSC AND ATJI

Established in 1974 with the Legal Services Corporation Act (codified at 42 U.S.C. 2996 et seq.), the LSC is now the largest funder of civil legal aid programs for low-income Americans. The federally-funded LSC awards grants to legal service providers, conducts reviews, visits programs, provides training and technical assistance, and encourages partnerships and collaborations to promote access to justice. Affiliated organizations provide direct representation, clinics, advice and self-help materials, and referrals to other social service programs.

The LSC website is forthright about their inability to meet demand, noting that more than 1 in 5 Americans qualify for services, but affiliated organizations turn away half of those seeking help due to a lack of resources (LSC 2015). In 2001, LSC distributed 95% of funding to 136 programs with 900 offices (United States 2011, sec.

302), but the LSC website as of 2015 states that 90% of funding goes toward 134 programs with approximately 800 offices (LSC 2015). Legal aid providers faced with LSC funding cuts must finance services through other means or limit resources in a time when the demand for legal assistance is only increasing.

Organizations receiving financial support from the LSC are subject to certain federal restrictions, which apply to all legal work within the organization. In addition to stipulating a maximum income requirement for clients, restrictions prohibit LSC-funded organizations from representing incarcerated individuals and undocumented or other immigrants, and participating in cases involving abortion, eviction cases if a person has been charged with drug crimes related to sales, and class actions (Columbia 2014, 424-426). Considering that a majority of legal aid lawyers today work in LSC-funded programs (LSC 2009, 19-20), these rules severely limit opportunities to serve many low-income individuals with pressing legal needs. If affiliated organizations are actually entirely prevented from representing immigrants in any legal matter, this restricts options for approximately 80 million immigrants and their children living in the United States (Zong & Batalova 2015), leaving about ¼ of the total U.S. population with few choices but to hire an attorney or advocate for themselves.

The U.S. Department of Justice established the Access to Justice Initiative (hereinafter "ATJI," differentiating the Federal Initiative from the broader ATJ movement) in 2010 to increase access to counsel and legal assistance for those who cannot afford lawyers in civil and criminal cases. Projects focus on advancing statutory and policy changes to support legal aid services; promoting alternative solutions to legal problems; removing income, literacy, mobility, and language barriers; and expanding research on methods of closing the justice gap (United States Department of Justice 2015). The ATJI, much like the LSC, is charged with improving indigent defense, advancing civil representation for the middle class and poor, and focusing on the needs of the most vulnerable (United States 2011, 297). State commissions involved with the ATJ movement coordinate access to justice on the state level and collect information on funding sources for civil legal aid. As of 2014, 38 states have official Commissions. The American Bar Association (ABA) Resource Center for Access to Justice Initiatives maintains online resources and a directory of state

ATJ commissions (American Bar Association 2015) and also hosts a national meeting of state chairpersons.

The LSC and ATJI address equality concerns in the legal system but, as currently conceived, they are insufficient to close the justice gap alone. Services vary widely by state and jurisdiction, leaving residents in many areas without access to civil legal aid (Columbia 2014, 411). Although the U.S. has a surplus of lawyers, many of whom are unemployed or underemployed, relatively few attorneys focus on the low-income population. On average across the country, one legal aid attorney is available to serve 6,415 poor people. For those who are able to afford representation, one private attorney is available for every 429 people (LSC 2009, 22). Overall, ten times as many lawyers are representing the general U.S. population with incomes above LSC poverty guidelines than legal aid attorneys serving the low-income population (19-20). Although the LSC and ABA also support pro bono service by private lawyers, too few attorneys advocate for low-income clients. Put simply, although everyone is aware of the problem, no one has a funding solution that will allow either LSC to help everyone eligible for its assistance, or ATJI to provide representation for other low-income people in need.

Columbia Law School's Human Rights Clinic suggests that in order to close the justice gap, the government must support ongoing research, fully fund LSC and ATJ initiatives, lift LSC restrictions, provide ATJI leadership and resources on state and federal levels, and establish the civil right to counsel — especially in cases such as immigration proceedings where liberty and fundamental human needs are at stake (Columbia 2014, 415). However, as one critic wrote in 2003, years before the U.S. economic recession, "there will never be enough affordable legal services to meet the demand for full legal representation for all individuals. Given existing budgetary restraints, a 400% increase in funding for legal services is highly unlikely. Similarly unlikely is a dramatic increase in pro bono activity by lawyers, a dramatic decrease in legal fees, or a return to the barter system of an earlier era in which clients could pay for legal assistance with their own goods and services" (Hannaford-Agor 2003, 9). Realistic proposals might consider appropriate ways to assist individuals advocating for themselves in legal matters, by offering a range of resources and services other than direct assistance from an attorney. If direct representation and economic aid are not viable options, self-represented litigants at a minimum need information about legal procedures and the court system. Public law libraries not only provide access to reliable and up-to-date legal materials, they also support patrons through reference and other services. Instead of working exclusively toward the ideal of civil representation for all, legal aid providers and law library initiatives should focus on simplifying court procedures and making legal information more available and comprehensible for the average layperson.

Types of Law Libraries Open to the Public

As neutral providers of legal information, law libraries play an active role in facilitating access to justice. The American Association of Law Libraries states that "[a]ccess to justice includes affordable legal services; readily available legal information and forms; the ability to bring a case to trial without hiring an attorney; the unbundling of legal services; fair treatment and equality in the justice system regardless of social standing; and confidence that the outcome will be fair and just" (AALL 2014, 5). The concept of ATJ as envisioned by AALL supports the fundamental values of LSC and ATJI, but it also minimizes the role of attorneys in legal proceedings and defines a responsibility to provide public access to legal information and forms. By bringing attention away from traditional legal aid services and toward information access, AALL begins to carve a niche for law librarians in a justice movement led by lawyers and government agencies.

Although some law librarians are also attorneys, the duties of a librarian exclude the practice of law. Librarians organize information for easy retrieval, help patrons identify and use relevant information, and act as translators between systems (Zorza 2012, 16). Not all libraries are open to the public, but those that are generally fit into three categories: public; academic; and state, court, and county libraries. Research materials in law firms are rarely, if ever, available to SRLs, although some firm librarians do play an active role in pro bono services and the ATJ movement. This chapter confines its scope to libraries with public access.

Public libraries are the most accessible option, but many do not maintain robust legal collections in print. As more primary legal information becomes available for free through state websites and online databases, libraries that provide basic access to the internet can still facilitate legal research. Patrons may find forms, court rules, brochures, and other self-help materials through court websites and centralized state ATJ websites if they are maintained for the particular jurisdiction. While many public librarians do have experience answering common legal questions, some have voiced discomfort about crossing the boundary between reference service and unauthorized practice of law (AALL 2014, 11). This boundary is also frustrating for patrons.

Academic law libraries are generally affiliated with public or private law schools.[1] Policies vary between institutions and may restrict public access to the legal collection during certain hours, require an appointment with a researcher, or entirely exclude SRLs from the legal collection (AALL 2014, 7). Some academic law libraries offer extensive legal services for the surrounding community such as hosting legal clinics, creating partnerships with surrounding organizations, or conducting training programs for public librarians (8).

Some states require a public law library in the courthouse, some may provide for courthouse libraries not open to the public, and some states have law libraries but lack additional funding for access to justice programs (AALL 2014, 6). The range of services provided by state, court, and county law libraries depends heavily on political governance, funding, and geographical location.[2] Some law libraries offer SRL assistance through self-help centers. The AALL State, Court, County Law Libraries Special Interest Section developed sets of "Standards" for County and Appellate Courts regarding physical space, services, and collection policies. AALL urges regional law library groups to supplement these "Standards" with additional lists of recommended state resources for academic and public library collections.

---

1   Washburn University maintains an index to law school libraries and catalogs across the U.S. and Canada ("Law School Library & State Law Library Catalogs").

2   Washburn University also maintains an index to state, court, and county law libraries across the U.S. ("State, Court, and County Law Libraries").

FEDERAL DEPOSITORY LIBRARIES

As the "largest publisher in the world," the U.S. Government Publishing Office (GPO) publishes primary legal texts and facts about government structure and operations. The Federal Depository Library Program (FDLP) was established to distribute government documents among designated public, academic, and law libraries at no cost. Depository libraries provide free public access and professional assistance for Federal Depository collections. A searchable "Federal Depository Libraries" interface is available online to locate participating libraries.

Legal requirements for the program are set forth in 44 U.S.C. §§ 1901-1916. These statutes mandate the distribution and delivery of specific publications, including the U.S. House and Senate Journals, non-confidential Committee publications and reports, public bills, and resolutions. In return, participating depository libraries agree to catalog the documents, maintain the collection, have an additional collection of at least ten thousand books, and report to the Superintendent of Documents every two years. Some libraries are required to keep publications open to the public for five years, others retain them permanently in tangible formats. Federal Depository libraries receive free access to select agency subscription databases (Federal Depository Libary Program 2015). As the GPO shifts to publishing more historical and up-to-the-minute information online through government websites like GPO.gov and Congress.gov, it will be interesting to see the effect on participating FDLP libraries.

Depository libraries have supplemental collections varying in size and utility, and the Depository program does not provide funding for public access to Lexis or Westlaw. Although the U.S. Government is the world's largest publisher, legal professionals primarily use resources published by other private companies like Bloomberg BNA, LexisNexis, West, Thomson Reuters, Wolters Kluwer, and others. Beginning in the late nineteenth century, these publishers "took public domain information and edited, indexed, packaged, and marketed it for a targeted (and well-paying) audience of legal professionals who could support the creation of this 'refined' product. But one consequence of targeting such a small audience was that little of this information was available to ordinary citizens" (Wise & Schauer 2007, 279). Subscription costs for legal databases such as

Lexis or Westlaw are beyond many library budgets, but conducting case law research without them is difficult. A large amount of public information has been repackaged and privatized by companies that charge access fees and have the power to exclude the average citizen and public libraries from their databases. Even texts in the public domain, such as statutes, regulations, and court decisions, can be nearly impossible to find through free resources and usually lack annotations or citator services to determine whether material is still valid. The FDLP offers an opportunity for participating libraries to maintain a basic collection of primary federal resources, but patrons also need annotated case law and other materials specific to their jurisdiction, along with secondary resources to help them understand the information. Most of these materials are only published by for-profit companies, and the cost of maintaining database access or print updates can be prohibitive.

INFORMATION ACCESS VS. LEGAL ADVICE

Access to legal and government documents online should logistically translate to a system-wide ease of use, but the fluidity of the law and complexity of legal research present challenges beyond mere information access. Libraries that prominently feature subject guides and materials written for non-attorneys make entire collections more accessible and comprehensible for those without prior legal knowledge. In order to mitigate the digital divide, libraries should provide user-friendly hardware and software, feature a mix of print and electronic resources that are intuitive to use and written with simple language, organize information through a single gateway or website, and allow patrons enough time on computer stations (Zorza 2012, 32-33). Librarians can also explain basic computer concepts to patrons who lack experience with internet search engines and legal databases, and provide supplemental materials for those unfamiliar with legal terminology.

Law librarians may educate researchers about using legal information, but cannot provide direct representation or legal advice. Lawyers cannot form an attorney-client relationship with patrons while working as law librarians. Although public librarians report frequent concerns with overstepping the line from legal reference to legal advice, most law librarians are familiar with appropriate methods of using information to address SRL issues (AALL 2014, 11). Librarians overstep the boundary into unauthorized practice if they state their personal opinions on a case, predict likely outcomes, recommend a choice of action when multiple courses are possible, suggest tactical steps, help develop an argument, or judge what actions will be most effective in court proceedings (Zorza 2012, 24). Law librarians are trained to provide generic, neutral information that is not specific to the individual's case, and to further direct patrons to resources that address their specific questions.

As a prolific writer on the limitations of unauthorized practice, Richard Zorza's touchstones for librarian neutrality are that "in order to be considered neutral, the same information could be given to all sides, the information and discussion is not confidential, no independent judgment is being exercised in the finding of the information, and there is no expectation of loyalty or ongoing service" (9). Such guidelines help librarians define their roles, but restrictions can change over time and vary between institutions. Telling patrons what forms to file was once considered unauthorized practice, but librarians and court staff may now explain what steps need to be completed in the context of the case as long as the information is factual rather than strategic (9). However, some libraries and courts still discourage staff from identifying the appropriate forms to file. Written library policies should clarify the librarian's responsibilities under specific guidelines, and written or verbal disclaimers distinguishing legal information from advice can also help manage patron expectations.

LIBRARY SERVICES FOR SELF-REPRESENTED LITIGANTS

Law libraries report a changing patron base over recent years, with visits by lawyers and court staff decreasing while more public and SRL patrons visit the library to address their legal needs (Zorza 2012, 1). Zorza calls on libraries to join the justice system in taking more responsibility for systemic change: "As the justice system re-orients itself from one only designed to decide cases to one responsible for providing access to justice for all, and as technologies transform access to legal information, law libraries will have no choice but to re-assess, re-design, and re-purpose towards a broad access to justice mission" (4). As principal providers of legal information, libraries should take an active role in promoting self-help centers and creating more resources to address legal needs of the public.

The AALL Access to Justice Special Committee published a 2014 report, *Law Libraries and Access to Justice*, that outlines some general criteria and proposes suggestions for three levels of service typically offered by law libraries (28-31). At the most basic level, libraries provide space, books, and computers with internet access. These 'Basic Level' law libraries can address SRL needs by promoting state and county websites and ensuring that their computer software supports any e-filing and document assembly programs used by local and state courts. Public access to computers, phones, copiers, printers, and scanners should be free or available for a moderate fee. Print collections should also include plain-language forms and basic materials written for SRLs.

To reach users outside the library, librarians can develop or maintain a collection of digital materials on the library website or through a centralized state ATJ website if one exists. State libraries and legal aid providers can compile self-help resources and directories online using LSC-created legal information gateways, available through lawhelp.org. Librarians should take the initiative to learn about local legal aid services in order to refer patrons to outside organizations if their needs cannot be met at the library (AALL 2014, 28-29).

The Self Represented Litigation Network found that 84% of libraries answering a 2014 programming survey provided some level of service to SRLs. Of these, 97% offer public computers with Internet access (SRLN 2014, 3) and 90% provide traditional reference and computerized legal research for the public. More than 80% of libraries with reference services for the public offer phone reference and a print collection for non-lawyers, and 90% give referrals to outside organizations. Others have e-mail reference, print or electronic research guides, and maintain websites intended for SRLs. Survey results indicate that a vast majority of law libraries are offering at least a basic level of service for SRL patrons.

'Intermediate Level' law libraries offer additional services alongside basic collections and access to technology. They may host clinics, lawyer-in-the-library programs, or Continuing Legal Education courses for attorneys or the public (AALL 2014, 29). Some librarians take on roles as information creators, rather than just curators, by working with the court and other stakeholders to develop plain language forms or interactive forms. Creating such materials does not constitute unauthorized practice. Zorza explains, "[t]he very act of turning legal knowledge into online information or tools can help make that information more appropriate for non-lawyer use. If answers or choices are standardized, there is no longer individual judgment being applied, and the service becomes informational" (2012, 11). The LSC and State Justice Institute jointly developed tools to facilitate document assembly programs through LawHelp Interactive, available at lawhelpinteractive.com (2009, 35-36).

Data regarding court form provision shows that 95% of responding law libraries have court forms available in print or online. Two-thirds of these forms also include instructions, but only 11% of responding libraries write the instructions themselves. Comparatively few libraries offer further assistance in helping patrons understand or fill out forms. One-third have forms in plain English but few are printed in multiple languages, leaving non-English speakers with little recourse for understanding the few standardized materials available to them (SRLN 2014, 2). However, over 35% of libraries with self-help centers offer some materials in multiple languages, such as books and brochures, and about 20% have bi-lingual staff, provisions for interpreters, or access to a language line (3). Although 22% of responding libraries provide direct access to document assembly or interactive forms, less than 15% create forms, write instructions, or assist litigants in filling them out (2). SRL patrons do have access to limited forms through the library but will not necessarily receive help in choosing and completing them appropriately.

Libraries with 'Advanced Level' services offer extensive legal assistance to all patrons through self-help centers, some of which are directed by attorneys on the library staff, or the library may route patrons directly to attorneys or other representatives from legal service organizations for limited representation or unbundled services. These 'advanced' services described by AALL are free from the many limitations of other self-help centers, such as income restrictions, delays in securing meetings, limits on time spent with an attorney, and residency issues. Few, if any, libraries provide this level of service, and AALL presents it as a goal or "self-help center of the future" where "all people who need legal assistance can meet with an attorney within appropriate time frames to not only help them begin addressing their legal needs but also to provide assistance in completion of the legal process" (2014, 31). Such point-of-need attention differs from the private attorney-client relationship found in full, direct representation. If self-help center programming includes attorney consultations, the library should utilize an open space plan to give the impression of security and neutrality while underscoring the limited and non-private relationship between the staff and public (Zorza 2012, 2).

Indeed, some library self-help centers offer direct services similar to this model. Results of the SRLN survey showed that about 35% of respondents have self-help centers, with most located within state and county law libraries and others run by and located in outside organizations with library support (SRLN 2014, 3). Locations should be within easy access of the court and highly visible to new clients (Zorza 2012, 29-30). Collaborative models in which the law library supports an externally-located center are most common, but other self-help programs are fully operated and run by the law library. A small number of respondents described centers located within the law library but administered by court personnel or another organization. All of these programs offer a limited scope of assistance, depend on referrals and websites for marketing, and reported little involvement by state or local bar associations (SRLN 2014, 5). Self-help centers appear to be working toward the "Advanced Level' of service as envisioned by AALL but, perhaps unsurprisingly, at this point none are able to meet the full extent of legal needs within their community.

PARTNERSHIPS, TRIAGE AND REFERRAL

The law library can leverage its presence in the community as a neutral information provider, access point, and intermediary between members of the public, courts, and legal aid organizations. Participation in state ATJ Commissions increases opportunities for librarians to network and form partnerships, participate in advocacy, learn more about courts and legal aid organizations, and connect the public with legal aid services through referrals (AALL 2014, 14-15). Law librarians in states without ATJ Commissions may find similar opportunities in local Bar associations or structured gatherings of legal service providers. As stakeholders in the justice system, law librarians should take initiative in all ways possible to advocate for libraries, make their perspectives heard, and be recognized as key members in the ATJ movement.

When planning and developing public services, librarians should first identify and involve potential community partners. Stakeholders may include attorneys, court staff, members of the judiciary, government representatives, community organizations, other local libraries, and SRLs themselves. In particular, self-help centers necessitate stakeholder input to develop a shared mission and vision, determine the community's needs, and identify services offered outside the library (Zorza 2012, 14). Partners should continue to help identify, create, support, and maintain program components over time. Involving collaborators from the project's inception facilitates the ongoing division of labor as the project grows in scope.

Feedback from stakeholders might also identify key services that the library can offer other organizations. For example, local public or academic librarians might request training in the legal collection, agree to collaborate on shared websites and programs, and promote advertising for law library services (SRLN 2014, 8). Legal aid organizations with limited space and resources could use library meeting rooms and equipment or free memberships and research assistance for staff, and might be willing to partner for grants and recommend referrals when appropriate. Many law libraries that have explicit relationships with state or local courts can also improve their services. Librarians could offer traditional reference and means for information access to court staff or local attorneys, provide referrals and triage through a self-help program, manage a website geared toward SRLs, create informational webinars, act as a distribution point for forms, host programs or workshops on legal topics, and provide computers with internet access to the public (7-8). Libraries offer a wide range of services regardless of patron income, many of which are not duplicated in other agencies (10-11). Expanding these services to first address the unmet needs of allies will raise awareness and support for a structured self-help center or triage program, and also help librarians achieve a central role in statewide ATJ Commissions.

Patrons are often referred from law libraries to legal aid organizations, or vice versa, for particular services. Zorza defines the concept of triage as the "ability to decide what people need to move forward, whether the library can provide it, and, if not, what alternative referral might be helpful" (2012, 18). Referrals often connect patrons with needed services, but if staff are ignorant of an organization's limitations they risk sending patrons on a fool's errand. Effective triage depends on personal intuition, awareness, and experience. Little has been written about triage or referral systems in court or legal aid locations, and none within the law library context. No standard protocol provides guidelines or best practices (18-19). In order to recommend appropriate legal materials, librarians must have a firm grasp on the law itself, what existing literature is most appropriate to the issue, and how legal problems interrelate (23). To refer patrons elsewhere, librarians also need to know what services are provided by each organization, contact information, any client restrictions, intake procedures, and whether the organization is presently accepting new clients. No central resource pulls such information together, but librarians should take the initiative to stay abreast of changes to the legal landscape as they develop. This is often achieved through a combination of online research and word of mouth, so it is essential to maintain involvement through meetings, list-servs, and personal communication within the legal community.

INNOVATIVE LIBRARY SERVICES FOR CHANGING TIMES

Technology opens new avenues of communication with patrons and partners, and offers libraries the potential to provide a range of services to a larger constituency at low cost. While most library websites disseminate basic information about collections and services, some also provide public portals to facilitate effective online research. Centralized state websites run by an ATJ Commission, LawHelp.org, court, or the law library itself can act as pathfinders to link users with reputable sources of legal information across a wide jurisdiction. However, librarians should not assume that all patrons have home internet access and computer literacy, and policies must also allow users sufficient time on public terminals. Subscribing to proprietary legal databases can reduce paper subscriptions, minimize collections and lessen reliance on physical space, cut down on the staff workload of filing and cataloguing print updates, and allow for more efficient research (Zorza 2012, 11-12). Librarians should remain patient and receptive if patrons require extra time or explanation while using computer terminals.

Websites, online reference services, and databases have long been used by law libraries to reach patrons, but emerging technologies are also changing the ways litigants file court documents. Zorza highlights benefits for librarians, noting that "[t]echnology makes low marginal cost access to resources possible, and facilitates tools that allow expertise to be provided to patrons even when staff are generalists (such as: online diagnosis and document assembly)" (2012. 2). Standardized forms are slowly becoming available on more court websites, and document assembly systems such as LawHelp Interactive can generate completed forms from a series of questions and answers. Some jurisdictions that previously offered e-filing only for attorneys now provide the service for all litigants. Law libraries may be required to update computer software and offer assistance in using the interfaces as e-filing technology becomes more prevalent (20). Librarians must be cognizant of emerging technology in the justice system and continue advocating for the public to make sure it is appropriate and accessible for all litigants.

At this point no model or standard governs library self-help centers (Zorza 2012, 1) and consistent evaluation measures for exemplary practices are yet to be established (10). Until then, self-help centers can implement their own follow-up diagnostics as well as "set goals, establish metrics, and obtain input and perspective from a wide variety of users and constituencies to determine and affirm that they are meeting the needs of all of their patrons" (3). It goes without saying that all library services should be periodically reviewed to ensure they are meeting patron expectations, particularly services intended for the public. Eventually, the AALL and law libraries as a whole should agree on standards for practice and evaluation of library self-help programs. The right standards will help libraries to do everything they can for SRLs struggling to achieve justice in complex systems that often fail to meet their own stated ideals of providing justice for all. Ultimately, the severe shortfall in funding for legal services for low-income people must be overcome, and biases toward immigrants and similar groups must give way so that services can be apportioned to all who need them. Until then, libraries have an important role to play in helping SRLs to do everything they can to achieve justice for themselves and their families.

Works Cited

American Association of Law Libraries. 1999. "AALL Ethical Principles." http://www.aallnet.org/mm/Leadership-Governance/policies/PublicPolicies/policy-ethics.html.

American Association of Law Libraries, Special Committee on Access to Justice. 2014. *Law Libraries and Access to Justice, A Report of the American Association of Law Libraries Special Committee on Access to Justice.* http://www.aallnet.org/mm/Publications/products/atjwhitepaper.pdf.

American Association of Law Libraries, State, Court, and County Law Libraries Special Interest Section. 2015. "Standards." Accessed April 24. http://www.aallnet.org/sections/sccll/leadership/Standards

.American Bar Association. 2015. "State ATJ Commission Directory." Accessed April 21. http://www.americanbar.org/groups/legal_aid_indigent_defendants/initiatives/resource_center_for_access_to_justice/state_atj_commissions.html.

Columbia Law School Human Rights Clinic. 2014. "Access to Justice: Ensuring Meaningful Access to Counsel in Civil Cases." *Syracuse Law Review* 64 (3): 409-445. Columbia Law School. http://web.law.columbia.edu/human-rights-institute/publications.

DeNavas-Walt, Carmen, and Bernadette D. Proctor. 2014. "Income and Poverty in the United States: 2013." U.S. Census Bureau. http://www.census.gov/library/publications/2014/demo/p60-249.html.

Depository Library Program, 44 U.S.C. §§ 1901 et seq. 2006.

Federal Depository Library Program. 2015. "Collections and Databases." Accessed April 22. http://www.fdlp.gov/requirements-guidance/collections-and-databases.

—-. 2015. "Federal Depository Libraries."Accessed April 22. http://www.fdlp.gov/about-the-fdlp/federal-depository-libraries.

Hannaford-Agor, Paula L. 2003. "Helping the Pro Se Litigant: A Changing Landscape." *Court Review* 8 (Winter): 8-16. HeinOnline.

Legal Services Corporation. 2014. *2013 Legal Services Corporation By the Numbers: The Data Underlying Legal Aid Programs.* http://www.lsc.gov/about/lsc-numbers-2013.

—-. 2015. "About LSC." Accessed April 17. http://www.lsc.gov/about/what-is-lsc

—-. 2009. *Documenting the Justice Gap In America: The Current Unmet Civil Legal Needs of Low-Income Americans.* Washington, D.C.: Legal Services Corporation. American Bar Association. http://www.americanbar.org/content/dam/aba/migrated/marketresearch/PublicDocuments/JusticeGaInAmerica2009.authcheckdam.pdf.

Legal Services Corporation Act, 42 U.S.C. 2996 et seq. 2006. National Legal Aid and Defender Association. 2011. "History of Right to Counsel." http://www.nlada.org/About/About_HistoryDefender.

Self Represented Litigation Network, Law Librarians Working Group. 2014. *Library Self-Help Programs and Services: A Survey of Law Library Programs for Self-Represented Litigants, Including Self-Help Centers.* http://www.selfhelpsupport.org/surveys/.

United States. 2011. *Fourth Periodic Report of the United States of America to the United Nations Committee on Human Rights Concerning the International Covenant on Civil and Political Rights*, Article 14, U.N. Doc. CCPR/C/USA/4 (Dec. 30, 2011). http://www.state.gov/j/drl/rls/179781.htm.

United States Department of Justice. 2015. "The Access to Justice Initiative." Accessed April 17. http://www.justice.gov/atj.

Washburn University School of Law. 2015. "Law School Library & State Law Library Catalogs." Accessed April 21. http://www. washlaw.edu/lawcat/index.html.

—-. 2015. "State, Court, and County Law Libraries." Accessed April 21. http://www.washlaw.edu/statecourtcounty/.

Wise, Virginia J. and Frederick Schauer. 2007. "Legal Information as Social Capital." *Law Library Journal* 99 (2): 267-283. HeinOnline.

Zong, Jie and Jeanne Batalova. 2015. "Frequently Requested Statistics on Immigrants and Immigration in the United States." Migration Policy Institute. http://www.migrationpolicy. org/article/frequently-requested-statistics-immigrants-and-immigration-united-states.

Zorza, Richard. 2012. *The Sustainable 21ˢᵗ Century Law Library: Vision, Deployment and Assessment for Access to Justice.* Zorza Associates. http://zorza.net/LawLibrary.pdf.

Author Biographies

BALES, STEPHEN E: Stephen Bales is an Associate Professor and Humanities and Social Sciences Librarian at Texas A&M University Libraries. He received his PhD. In Communication & Information from the University of Tennessee, Knoxville. His research interests include the history and philosophy of library and information science, professional identity in library and information science, and political economy and the academic library.

BIRD, AMANDA: Amanda Bird holds an MLIS degree from Dalhousie University and works at an urban public library in Alberta, Canada. She is passionate about community-led library service, and is concerned about the precarious employment practices of library systems in Canada.

BARRIAGE, SARAH: Sarah Barriage, BA, MLIS is a PhD candidate in the School of Communication & Information at Rutgers, The State University of New Jersey. Before entering doctoral studies, Sarah worked as a public services librarian at an academic library in Alberta, Canada. Her research interests involve the incorporation of a social justice perspective to both practice and research in library and information science.

CANNON, BRADEN: Braden Cannon is an archivist at a public archives in Alberta, Canada and holds an MLIS degree from Dalhousie University. He is a union steward for the Alberta Union of Provincial Employees, a founding member of the Edmonton branch of the Progressive Librarians Guild, and a member of the Industrial Workers of the World.

CARRUTHERS, ALEXANDRA: Alexandra Carruthers has a Masters in Library and Information Studies and a Masters in English from the University of Alberta. She is currently the Digital Public Spaces Librarian at Edmonton Public Library. The through line of her intellectual and professional endeavors is an interest in collectivity and community building.

McEACHRON, PEGGY: Peggy McEachreon BA MA MLIS AHIP, is the Librarian Educator responsible for Remote Access for the Nova Scotia Health Authority library service. Peggy has worked as a health sciences librarian for over 2 years now, and has previous experience in both public and academic libraries. Health sciences librarianship brings together many of her interests and passions including health research, health advocacy, outreach, and information access advocacy. Peggy believes in empowering others through education and information sharing because this increases people's confidence which inspires them to take leadership roles. A culture of well-informed leaders will contribute to a better healthcare system, and a better world. Peggy also enjoys running, hiking, drumming, and singing.

SAMEK, TONI: Dr. Toni Samek is a Professor and Chair at the School of Library and Information Studies, University of Alberta. Toni twice convened the Canadian Library Association's Advisory Committee on Intellectual Freedom, served two consecutive terms on the Canadian Association of University Teachers' Academic Freedom and Tenure Committee, and is currently on the Advisory Board of Canada's Centre for Free Expression.

SIAS, CAREY: Carey Sias is the Systems Librarian at Jenkins Law Library in Philadelphia, where she has worked in Systems and in the Reference Department since 2010. She teaches Continuing Legal Education classes and leads outreach initiatives to increase library services for *pro se* patrons. Ms. Sias has served as Secretary and Treasurer on the Board of the Greater Philadelphia Law Library Association and is an active member of the Philadelphia Bar Association›s Delivery of Legal Services committee. She holds a Bachelor›s of Arts degree from Macalester College and a Master's of Library and Information Science from Drexel University.

WRIGHT, STEVEN: Steve Wright works in the Faculty of Information Technology, Monash University. His current research centres on community archives, and the creation and use of documents in social movements.

INDEX

www.ingramcontent.com/pod-product-compliance
Lightning Source LLC
Chambersburg PA
CBHW071025280326
41935CB00011B/1476